United States Government Accountability Office

Report to the Secretary of the Treasury

I0455435

December 2013

# FINANCIAL AUDIT

# IRS's Fiscal Years 2013 and 2012 Financial Statements

GAO-14-169

# GAO
# Highlights

Highlights of GAO-14-169, a report to the Secretary of the Treasury

# FINANCIAL AUDIT

## IRS's Fiscal Years 2013 and 2012 Financial Statements

## Why GAO Did This Study

In accordance with the authority granted by the Chief Financial Officers Act of 1990, GAO annually audits IRS's financial statements to determine whether (1) the financial statements are fairly presented and (2) IRS management maintained effective internal control over financial reporting. GAO also tests IRS's compliance with selected provisions of applicable laws, regulations, contracts, and grant agreements.

IRS's tax collection activities are significant to overall federal receipts, and the effectiveness of its financial management is of substantial interest to Congress and the nation's taxpayers.

## What GAO Recommends

Based on prior financial statement audits, GAO made numerous recommendations to IRS to address internal control deficiencies. GAO will continue to monitor and will report separately on IRS's progress in implementing prior recommendations that remain open. Consistent with past practice, GAO will also be separately reporting on the new internal control deficiencies identified in this year's audit, and providing IRS recommendations for corrective actions to address them.

In commenting on a draft of this report, IRS stated that it would continue to increase its focus on information security and internal controls while improving financial reporting.

View GAO-14-169. For more information, contact Cheryl E. Clark at (202) 512-3406 or clarkce@gao.gov.

## What GAO Found

In GAO's opinion, the Internal Revenue Service's (IRS) fiscal years 2013 and 2012 financial statements are fairly presented in all material respects. However, in GAO's opinion, IRS did not maintain effective internal control over financial reporting as of September 30, 2013, because of a continuing material weakness in internal control over unpaid tax assessments. GAO's tests of IRS's compliance with selected provisions of applicable laws, regulations, contracts, and grant agreements detected no reportable instances of noncompliance in fiscal year 2013.

The material weakness in internal control over unpaid tax assessments was primarily caused by financial system limitations and data entry errors that rendered IRS's system unable to readily distinguish between taxes receivable, compliance assessments, and write-offs in order to properly classify these components for financial reporting purposes. These deficiencies necessitated the use of a compensating estimation process to determine the amount of taxes receivable, the most material asset on IRS's balance sheet. Serious control deficiencies related to unpaid tax assessments are likely to continue to exist until IRS significantly enhances the capabilities of the systems it uses to account for unpaid tax assessments, and improves controls over the recording of information in taxpayer accounts so that reliable transaction-based balances for taxes receivable can be ultimately recorded in the general ledger.

During fiscal year 2013, IRS continued to make important progress in addressing deficiencies in internal control over its financial reporting systems. However, new and continuing deficiencies in internal control that GAO identified over information security, including missing security updates, insufficient monitoring of financial reporting systems, and weak encryption for authentication, constituted a significant deficiency in IRS's internal control. Until IRS fully addresses existing control deficiencies over its financial reporting systems, there is an increased risk that its financial and taxpayer data will remain vulnerable to inappropriate and undetected use, modification, or disclosure.

In addition to its internal control deficiencies, IRS faces significant ongoing financial management challenges associated with (1) safeguarding the large volume of sensitive hard copy taxpayer receipts and related information, and (2) its exposure to significant improper refunds from identity theft.

# Contents

**Abbreviations**

| | |
|---|---|
| CFO | Chief Financial Officer |
| FASAB | Federal Accounting Standards Advisory Board |
| FMFIA | Federal Managers' Financial Integrity Act of 1982 |
| IRS | Internal Revenue Service |
| MD&A | Management Discussion and Analysis |
| RSI | required supplementary information |

GAO U.S. GOVERNMENT ACCOUNTABILITY OFFICE

441 G St. N.W.
Washington, DC 20548

December 12, 2013

The Honorable Jacob J. Lew
Secretary of the Treasury

Dear Mr. Secretary:

The accompanying report presents the results of our audits of the fiscal years 2013 and 2012 financial statements of the Internal Revenue Service (IRS). Specifically, we found

- the financial statements are presented fairly, in all material respects, in accordance with U.S. generally accepted accounting principles;
- IRS's internal control over financial reporting was not effective as of September 30, 2013, because of a continuing material weakness[1] in internal control over unpaid tax assessments; and
- no reportable noncompliance in fiscal year 2013 with the laws, regulations, contracts, and grant agreements we tested.

This report also provides a discussion of a continuing significant deficiency[2] in IRS's internal control over financial reporting systems that we believe merits the attention of those charged with governance of IRS. We will be separately reporting more detailed information to IRS concerning the material weakness and significant deficiency along with any new recommended corrective actions. In addition, this report discusses ongoing financial management challenges that IRS faces associated with its (1) continued responsibility to safeguard hard copy taxpayer receipts and information, and (2) exposure to significant improper refunds from identity theft.

---

[1]A material weakness is a deficiency, or combination of deficiencies, in internal control over financial reporting, such that there is a reasonable possibility that a material misstatement of the entity's financial statements will not be prevented, or detected and corrected, on a timely basis. A deficiency in internal control exists when the design or operation of a control does not allow management or employees, in the normal course of performing their assigned functions, to prevent, or detect and correct, misstatements on a timely basis.

[2]A significant deficiency is a deficiency, or a combination of deficiencies, in internal control that is less severe than a material weakness, yet important enough to merit the attention of those charged with governance.

We performed our audit in accordance with authority granted by the Chief Financial Officers Act of 1990, as expanded by the Government Management Reform Act of 1994.

We are sending copies of this report to the Chairman and Vice Chairman of the Joint Committee on Taxation, the Chairmen and Ranking Members of the Senate Committee on Finance and the House Committee on Ways and Means, and other interested congressional committees and subcommittees. We are also sending copies of this report to the Acting Commissioner of Internal Revenue, the Director of the Office of Management and Budget, the Chairman of the IRS Oversight Board, and other interested parties. In addition, the report is available at no charge on the GAO website at http://www.gao.gov.

If you or your staff have any questions concerning this report, please contact me at (202) 512-3406 or clarkce@gao.gov. Contact points for our Offices of Congressional Relations and Public Affairs may be found on the last page of this report.

Sincerely yours,

*Cheryl E. Clark*

Cheryl E. Clark
Director
Financial Management and Assurance

## Independent Auditor's Report

To the Acting Commissioner of Internal Revenue

In our audits of the 2013 and 2012 financial statements of the Internal Revenue Service (IRS), we found

- the financial statements as of and for the fiscal years ended September 30, 2013, and 2012, are presented fairly, in all material respects, in accordance with U.S. generally accepted accounting principles;
- IRS's internal control over financial reporting was not effective as of September 30, 2013; and
- no reportable noncompliance for fiscal year 2013 with the provisions of applicable laws, regulations, contracts, and grant agreements we tested.

The following sections discuss in more detail (1) our report on the financial statements and internal control over financial reporting, which includes a matter of emphasis related to the tax gap and tax expenditures, other matters related to the required supplementary information (RSI)[1] and other information[2] included with the financial statements, and two significant financial management challenges confronting IRS related to safeguarding hard copy taxpayer receipts and information and its exposure to significant improper refunds from identity theft; (2) our report on compliance with laws, regulations, contracts, and grant agreements; and (3) IRS's comments on our evaluation.

---

[1]RSI is comprised of "Management's Discussion and Analysis," "Schedule of Budgetary Resources by Major Budget Accounts," and other RSI that is included with the financial statements.

[2]Other information is comprised of information included with the financial statements, other than the RSI and the auditor's report.

## Report on the Financial Statements and on Internal Control over Financial Reporting

In accordance with our authority granted by the Chief Financial Officers (CFO) Act of 1990, as expanded by the Government Management Reform Act of 1994,[3] we have audited the IRS's financial statements. IRS's financial statements comprise the balance sheets as of September 30, 2013, and 2012; the related statements of net cost, changes in net position, budgetary resources, and custodial activity for the fiscal years then ended; and the related notes to the financial statements. We have also audited IRS's internal control over financial reporting as of September 30, 2013, based on criteria established under 31 U.S.C. § 3512(c), (d), commonly known as the Federal Managers' Financial Integrity Act (FMFIA).

We conducted our audits in accordance with U.S. generally accepted government auditing standards. We believe that the audit evidence we obtained is sufficient and appropriate to provide a basis for our audit opinions.

## Management's Responsibility

IRS management is responsible for (1) the preparation and fair presentation of these financial statements in accordance with U.S. generally accepted accounting principles; (2) preparing, measuring, and presenting the RSI in accordance with the prescribed guidelines in U.S. generally accepted accounting principles; (3) preparing and presenting other information included in documents containing the audited financial statements and auditor's report, and ensuring the consistency of that information with the audited financial statements and the RSI; (4) maintaining effective internal control over financial reporting, including the design, implementation, and maintenance of internal control relevant to the preparation and fair presentation of financial statements that are free from material misstatement, whether due to fraud or error;

---

[3]See the CFO Act of 1990, Pub. L. No. 101-576, 104 Stat. 2838 (Nov. 15, 1990), codified, in relevant part, as amended, at 31 U.S.C. § 3521(g); see also the Government Management Reform Act of 1994, Pub. L. No. 103-356, 108 Stat. 3410 (Oct. 13, 1994), codified, in relevant part, as amended, at 31 U.S.C. § 3515(c). Under the authority of 31 U.S.C. § 3515, the Office of Management and Budget requires IRS to issue annual audited financial statements that are separate from those of the Department of the Treasury. Although the CFO Act designates the agency's inspector general, or where applicable, an independent external auditor, as the responsible auditor of an agency's financial statements, the act also gives GAO the authority to perform such audits at its discretion. Based on that authority, we audit IRS's financial statements because of the significance of IRS's tax collections to the consolidated financial statements of the U.S. government, which GAO is required to audit. See 31 U.S.C. § 331(e)(2).

(5) evaluating the effectiveness of internal control over financial reporting based on the criteria established under FMFIA; and (6) providing its assertion about the effectiveness of internal control over financial reporting as of September 30, 2013, based on its evaluation, included in the accompanying Management's Report on Internal Control over Financial Reporting in appendix I.

## Auditor's Responsibility

Our responsibility is to express an opinion on these financial statements and an opinion on IRS's internal control over financial reporting based on our audits. U.S. generally accepted government auditing standards require that we plan and perform the audits to obtain reasonable assurance about whether the financial statements are free from material misstatement, and whether effective internal control over financial reporting was maintained in all material respects. We are also responsible for applying certain limited procedures to the RSI and other information included with the financial statements.

An audit of financial statements involves performing procedures to obtain audit evidence about the amounts and disclosures in the financial statements. The procedures selected depend on the auditor's judgment, including the auditor's assessment of the risks of material misstatement of the financial statements, whether due to fraud or error. In making those risk assessments, the auditor considers internal control relevant to the entity's preparation and fair presentation of the financial statements in order to design audit procedures that are appropriate in the circumstances. An audit of financial statements also involves evaluating the appropriateness of the accounting policies used and the reasonableness of significant accounting estimates made by management, as well as evaluating the overall presentation of the financial statements. An audit of internal control over financial reporting includes obtaining an understanding of internal control over financial reporting, assessing the risk that a material weakness exists, evaluating the design and operating effectiveness of internal control over financial reporting based on the assessed risk, and testing relevant internal control over financial reporting. Our audit of internal control also considered the entity's process for evaluating and reporting on internal control over financial reporting based on criteria established under FMFIA. Our audits also included performing such other procedures as we considered necessary in the circumstances.

We did not evaluate all internal controls relevant to operating objectives as broadly established under FMFIA, such as those controls relevant to preparing performance information and ensuring efficient operations. We limited our internal control testing to testing controls over financial reporting. Our internal control testing was for the purpose of expressing an opinion on whether effective internal control over financial reporting was maintained, in all material respects. Consequently, our audit may not identify all deficiencies in internal control over financial reporting that are less severe than a material weakness.[4]

## Definitions and Inherent Limitations of Internal Control over Financial Reporting

An entity's internal control over financial reporting is a process effected by those charged with governance, management, and other personnel, the objectives of which are to provide reasonable assurance that (1) transactions are properly recorded, processed, and summarized to permit the preparation of financial statements in accordance with U.S. generally accepted accounting principles, and assets are safeguarded against loss from unauthorized acquisition, use, or disposition, and (2) transactions are executed in accordance with laws governing the use of budget authority and with other applicable laws, regulations, contracts, and grant agreements that could have a direct and material effect on the financial statements.

Because of its inherent limitations, internal control over financial reporting may not prevent, or detect and correct, misstatements due to fraud or error. We also caution that projecting any evaluation of effectiveness to future periods is subject to the risk that controls may become inadequate because of changes in conditions, or that the degree of compliance with the policies or procedures may deteriorate.

## Opinion on Financial Statements

In our opinion, IRS's financial statements present fairly, in all material respects, its financial position as of September 30, 2013, and 2012, and its net cost of operations, changes in net position, budgetary resources, and custodial activity for the fiscal years then ended in accordance with U.S. generally accepted accounting principles.

---

[4]A material weakness is a deficiency, or combination of deficiencies, in internal control over financial reporting, such that there is a reasonable possibility that a material misstatement of the entity's financial statements will not be prevented, or detected and corrected, on a timely basis. A deficiency in internal control exists when the design or operation of a control does not allow management or employees, in the normal course of performing their assigned functions, to prevent, or detect and correct, misstatements on a timely basis.

However, misstatements may nevertheless occur in other financial information reported by IRS and not be detected as a result of the internal control deficiencies described in this report.

## Emphasis of Matter

In accordance with federal accounting standards, the financial statements do not include an estimate of the dollar amount of taxes that are owed to the federal government but have not been reported by taxpayers or identified through IRS's enforcement programs, often referred to as the tax gap, nor do they include information on tax expenditures.[5] Further details discussing the tax gap and tax expenditures, as well as the associated dollar amounts, are discussed in the other information included with the financial statements.

## Opinion on Internal Control over Financial Reporting

In our opinion, because of a material weakness in internal control over unpaid tax assessments,[6] IRS did not maintain, in all material respects, effective internal control over financial reporting as of September 30, 2013, and thus did not provide reasonable assurance that losses and misstatements that were material in relation to the financial statements would be prevented, or detected and corrected, on a timely basis. Our opinion is based on criteria established under FMFIA.

Despite the material weakness in IRS's internal control over unpaid tax assessments, IRS made necessary and appropriate adjustments to its records and was therefore able to prepare financial statements that were fairly presented in all material respects for fiscal years 2013 and 2012. However, the material weakness may adversely affect any decisions by IRS's management that are based, in whole or in part, on information that is inaccurate because of this weakness. The issues constituting this material weakness, which are discussed in more detail below, were also

---

[5]The estimated magnitude of the tax gap is based on a study conducted to measure the compliance rate of taxpayers based on an examination of a statistical sample of tax returns filed for tax year 2006. Tax expenditures represent the amount of revenue that the government forgoes resulting from federal tax law provisions that (1) allow a special exclusion, exemption, or deduction from gross income or (2) provide a special credit, preferential rate, or deferred tax liability.

[6]An unpaid tax assessment is a legally enforceable claim against a taxpayer and consists of taxes, penalties, and interest that have not been collected or abated (i.e., the tax assessment reduced by IRS).

disclosed by IRS in its fiscal year 2013 (1) FMFIA assurance statement to the Department of the Treasury and (2) Management's Report on Internal Control over Financial Reporting. We considered this material weakness in determining the nature, timing, and extent of our audit procedures on IRS's fiscal years 2013 and 2012 financial statements.

In addition, our fiscal year 2013 audit identified continuing and new deficiencies concerning IRS's financial reporting systems that, while not considered a material weakness, are important enough to merit the attention of those charged with governance of IRS. Therefore, we considered these remaining and new issues affecting IRS's internal control over financial reporting systems collectively to be a significant deficiency[7] in internal control in fiscal year 2013. This significant deficiency is discussed in more detail later in this report.

In addition to the material weakness and significant deficiency in internal control, we also identified other deficiencies in IRS's internal control over financial reporting that we do not consider to be material weaknesses or significant deficiencies. Nonetheless, these deficiencies warrant IRS management's attention. We have communicated these matters to IRS management and, where appropriate, will report on them separately.

## Material Weakness in Internal Control over Unpaid Tax Assessments

During fiscal year 2013, we continued to find serious deficiencies that affected IRS's management and reporting of unpaid tax assessments. Specifically, we continued to find (1) IRS's reported balances for taxes receivable and other unpaid assessments were not supported by its core general ledger system for tax transactions; (2) IRS's subsidiary ledger for unpaid tax assessments did not allow it to produce reliable, useful, and timely information with which to manage and report externally; and (3) IRS experienced errors in recording taxpayer information.

As we have reported in prior audits,[8] IRS's systems are not designed to provide the accurate, complete, and timely transaction-level financial

---

[7]A significant deficiency is a deficiency, or a combination of deficiencies, in internal control that is less severe than a material weakness, yet important enough to merit the attention of those charged with governance.

[8]GAO, *Financial Audit: IRS's Fiscal Years 2012 and 2011 Financial Statements*, GAO-13-120 (Washington, D.C.: Nov. 9, 2012).

information necessary to enable IRS to reliably classify and report unpaid tax assessment balances in accordance with federal accounting standards.[9] As a result, IRS's balance for federal taxes receivable,[10] which comprised over 80 percent of total assets reported on its fiscal year 2013 balance sheet, was not produced from its general ledger but rather is a product of a labor-intensive manual compensating estimation process. This compensating process involves a statistical sampling of data extracted from its master files[11] to estimate the year-end balances of (1) taxes receivable reported in its financial statements and the RSI and (2) compliance assessments and write-offs reported in the RSI. While IRS adjusted the gross taxes receivable balance in its general ledger based on the results of this estimation process, IRS could not trace adjusted account balances to its detailed supporting records. Specifically, because the adjusted tax receivable balance is the product of a statistical estimation process, IRS is not able to (1) identify which taxpayers owe the unpaid tax assessments summarized in the gross taxes receivable balance or how much each one owes or (2) trace transactions from the taxes receivable amount, through its general ledger system, and back to underlying transaction-level source documents. Such traceability is necessary to enable IRS to ensure that recorded transactions are complete, accurate, and supported by underlying records.

IRS has an automated system that functions as a subsidiary ledger for its unpaid tax assessment accounts by analyzing and recording unpaid tax assessments balances from its master files on a weekly basis to its

---

[9]Federal accounting standards classify unpaid tax assessments into one of the following three categories for reporting purposes: federal taxes receivable, compliance assessments, and write-offs. Federal taxes receivable are taxes due from taxpayers for which IRS can support the existence of a receivable through, for example, taxpayer agreement or a court ruling determining an assessment. Compliance assessments are proposed tax assessments where neither the taxpayer (when the right to disagree or object exists) nor the court has affirmed that the amounts are owed. Write-offs represent unpaid tax assessments for which IRS does not expect further collections because of factors such as the taxpayer's death, bankruptcy, or insolvency. Federal accounting standards only require federal taxes receivable, net of an allowance for uncollectble amounts, to be reported on the financial statements. See Statement of Federal Financial Accounting Standards No. 7, *Accounting for Revenue and Other Financing Sources and Concepts for Reconciling Budgetary and Financial Accounting*, May 10, 1996.

[10]IRS reports federal taxes receivable on its balance sheet, net of an allowance for amounts considered uncollectible.

[11]IRS's master files contain detailed records of taxpayer accounts.

general ledger by the various financial reporting categories (taxes receivable, compliance assessments, and write-offs).[12] However, because of systemic deficiencies, IRS cannot use its subsidiary ledger for recording transaction-based unpaid tax assessment information to its general ledger in a manner that ensures reliable internal and external reporting. Specifically, while the subsidiary ledger analyzes and classifies unpaid tax assessment balances from its master files into the various financial reporting categories, the analysis and classification continues to contain material inaccuracies because IRS's classification program was unable to sort through, identify, and analyze all the relevant transaction-level information required for proper classification, recording, and reporting. For example, when IRS records multiple tax assessments against a taxpayer, its system is currently unable to accurately distinguish among and separately classify the various assessments among the three financial reporting categories. In all but the simplest of taxpayer accounts, the subsidiary ledger is not designed to distinguish between tax assessments that have been agreed to by the taxpayer and therefore represent a tax receivable, and those that have not been agreed to by the taxpayer, which generally represent a compliance assessment. For more complex accounts, which included assessments in both categories, IRS's systems generally classify the entire account balance as either a taxes receivable or compliance assessment, depending on which assessment was larger.

In addition to limitations with its automated systems, IRS's management and reporting for unpaid tax assessments also continued to be hindered by inaccurate tax records. During our fiscal year 2013 audit, we found errors in taxpayer records resulting from IRS not recording information accurately. Such errors directly affect the accuracy of the unpaid tax assessment information being classified by its subsidiary ledger. For example, in one case we reviewed, IRS wrongly assessed a taxpayer a $3 million penalty for not including an additional form along with the

---

[12]IRS's Custodial Detailed Data Base functions as its subsidiary ledger for unpaid tax assessments by linking and classifying taxpayer account information from IRS's master files to its general ledger for tax-related transactions by the various financial reporting categories (taxes receivable, compliance assessments, and write-offs). IRS's general ledger, which maintains the taxes receivable-related balance in accordance with the *U.S. Government Standard General Ledger,* produces the taxes receivable information in its financial statements. While the master files contain detailed records of taxpayer accounts, the master files do not contain all the details necessary to properly classify or estimate collectability for unpaid tax assessment accounts.

taxpayer's tax return. IRS subsequently determined that the taxpayer was actually not required to file this additional form. However, this error resulted in IRS recording an erroneous taxes receivable amount of $3 million because the penalty was associated with the self-reported tax. In another example, IRS erroneously recorded an entry in a taxpayer's account indicating that the taxpayer was involved in litigation. In accordance with federal tax law and implementing IRS procedures, recording this litigation activity in the taxpayer's account suspended the statutory time period that IRS had to collect the outstanding tax debt on the account.[13] In this instance, the account balance should not have been included in IRS's records because the taxpayer was not involved in litigation so the statutory collection period for this taxpayer's account had already expired. Such errors that result in inaccurate tax records can cause frustration to taxpayers when they are erroneously billed for amounts that are not valid, thus placing an undue burden on taxpayers who were then compelled to prove that IRS was in error.

Current systemic limitations and errors that caused inaccurate tax records resulted in IRS having to make numerous adjustments as part of its process for estimating the balance of net taxes receivable and other unpaid tax assessments. When IRS identified misclassified unpaid tax assessments resulting from systemic limitations and errors similar to those described above when reviewing its sample of unpaid tax assessments, it recorded adjustments to the affected taxpayer account to reflect the correct value of that taxpayer account at the point in time that IRS sampled the account information. On the basis of a statistical projection of these individual adjustments, IRS had to make multibillion-dollar adjustments to the year-end balances of all three categories of unpaid assessments generated by its subsidiary ledger in order to produce reliable amounts for external reporting on its balance sheet and the RSI. Specifically, through its use of its statistical sampling and estimation process, IRS identified errors necessitating almost $11 billion in adjustments to the 2013 fiscal year-end gross taxes receivable balance produced by its subsidiary ledger. Therefore, absent the use of this statistical estimation process, the various unpaid assessment balances

---

[13]IRS has a statutory limitation on the length of time it can pursue unpaid taxes, generally 10 years from the date of the tax assessment. If, however, IRS timely commences litigation for the collection of the tax, then the statutory collection period shall be extended and shall not expire until the tax liability (or the judgment against the taxpayer arising from such liability) is satisfied or becomes unenforceable. See 26 U.S.C. § 6502.

produced by its subsidiary ledger would have been significantly inaccurate.

The cumulative impact of these continuing control deficiencies is such that a reasonable possibility exists that a material misstatement of IRS's financial statements would not be prevented, or detected and corrected, on a timely basis. Consequently, these control deficiencies collectively represent a material weakness in IRS's internal control over unpaid tax assessments. Because of this material weakness and the associated system deficiencies that existed during fiscal year 2013, IRS's financial management systems were unable to report financial information in accordance with federal accounting standards, and did not comply with federal financial management systems requirements as embodied in *Treasury Financial Manual* Bulletin No. 2013-11, Revised Federal Financial Management System Requirements for Fiscal 2013 Reporting.[14]

Based on our recommendations from prior audits, IRS has taken actions over the years to improve its management and reporting of unpaid tax assessments, including the phased-in implementation of its subsidiary ledger for unpaid taxes to enable it to analyze and classify unpaid tax assessments account balances from the master file into the various financial reporting categories. However, IRS's actions to date have not been effective at fully addressing all the issues that continue to cause a lack of transaction traceability and material inaccuracies produced by this subsidiary ledger. IRS has developed an action plan intended to address the systemic deficiencies involving unpaid assessments; however, the plan does not discuss all of the system enhancements that are needed to enable its subsidiary ledger to more accurately distinguish between the three categories of unpaid tax assessments so that reliable transaction-based balances for each are ultimately recorded in the general ledger. Therefore, it is unclear if IRS's proposed actions will fully address the system issues that cause significant inaccuracies in the unpaid tax assessments information IRS uses for financial reporting. In addition, IRS has not communicated to us any specific plans to address data entry

---

[14]*Treasury Financial Manual* Bulletin No. 2013-11, *Revised Federal Financial Management System Requirements for Fiscal 2013 Reporting* (Sept. 25, 2013). IRS's financial management systems (1) did not substantially comply with Federal Financial Management Systems Requirements or federal accounting standards, and (2) substantially complied with the *U.S. Government Standard General Ledger* at the transaction level.

errors that also affect the accuracy and proper classification of unpaid tax assessment amounts. Based on IRS's most recent response to our open recommendation concerning data entry errors, IRS has yet to identify the underlying control deficiencies that have impaired its ability to prevent, or detect and correct, inaccuracies or errors in taxpayer accounts on a timely basis.[15] These serious deficiencies in internal control over unpaid tax assessments are likely to continue to exist until IRS (1) significantly enhances the capabilities of the systems it uses for recording, classifying, and reporting unpaid tax assessments to more accurately distinguish the balances among the three categories of unpaid tax assessments and (2) improves controls over the recording of information in taxpayer accounts, so that reliable transaction-based balances for taxes receivable can be ultimately recorded in the general ledger.

## Significant Deficiency in Internal Control over Financial Reporting Systems

During fiscal year 2013, IRS continued to devote significant attention and resources to securing its information systems and protecting sensitive taxpayer and financial information. Key among its significant actions during fiscal year 2013 was to address a large number of system control deficiencies that we previously reported. IRS also implemented a new procurement system and upgraded software for its administrative accounting system. These actions are important steps toward improving the overall effectiveness of its information system controls and therefore the reliability of its financial data. However, the remaining deficiencies in information security, along with new deficiencies we identified during this year's audit and discuss further below, are important enough to merit the attention of those charged with governance of IRS and therefore represent a significant deficiency in IRS's internal control over financial reporting systems as of September 30, 2013.

One of the more serious deficiencies that remained throughout fiscal year 2013 was that IRS did not install appropriate security updates on certain databases and servers, which increased the risk that known information security vulnerabilities could be exploited. Another serious deficiency that continued to exist during fiscal year 2013 concerned IRS's lack of sufficient monitoring of internal and external system control activities supporting its financial reporting. This increased the risk that any

---

[15]GAO, *Management Report: Improvements Are Needed to Enhance the Internal Revenue Service's Internal Controls*, GAO-13-420R (Washington, D.C.: May 13, 2013).

deficiencies in internal control over these systems may not be timely detected, or that any resultant misstatements may not be timely detected or corrected, thereby hindering IRS's ability to effectively assess and respond to security risks.[16]

We previously reported that IRS had not established and implemented procedures to monitor internal control over externally controlled automated systems that were material to its financial reporting.[17] We recommended that IRS, among other actions, establish an agreement with each service provider to allow IRS personnel the access to information needed to evaluate the effectiveness of IRS's internal control. However, in fiscal year 2013 we found that while progress has been made, deficiencies in IRS's monitoring of internal control over these service organizations continued to exist. According to guidance to federal agencies concerning management's responsibility for internal control, user entities such as IRS have two options available to them to assess internal control over financial reporting at these entities: (1) obtain the results of an independent assessment of the service provider's internal control, or (2) perform tests of the service provider's controls.[18] However, only one of IRS's service provider's independent auditors produced a

---

[16]In addition to numerous in-house automated systems, IRS relies on external service organizations for significant aspects of its financial management activities. Services provided by an external service organization are considered to be part of a user entity's information system relevant to the user entity's financial reporting if the services affect classes of transactions that are significant to the user entity's financial statements. Accordingly, user entities should monitor the effectiveness of the internal control over the systems and services provided by the service organizations.

[17]GAO, *Management Report: Improvements Are Needed to Enhance the Internal Revenue Service's Internal Controls and Operating Effectiveness*, GAO-12-683R (Washington, D.C.: June 25, 2012). We would generally consider a system to be quantitatively material to financial reporting if it processes and/or reports a material dollar amount of the transactions that are included in agency internal and/or external financial reports during a reporting period. The assessment of the significance of a deficiency in the internal control over such a system may be elevated if it also exhibits qualitative characteristics, such as processing (1) an inordinately large volume of financial transactions, and/or (2) related sensitive information, the safeguarding of which is a matter of substantial concern to financial statement users.

[18]Office of Management and Budget, *Implementation Guide for OMB Circular A-123 Management's Responsibility for Internal Control, Appendix A, Internal Control Over Financial Reporting* (Washington, D.C.: July 2005).

report on its internal controls during fiscal year 2013.[19] For the remaining service providers, IRS relied upon its review of system documentation which was provided by service provider management. The preponderance of this documentation predated fiscal year 2013. In some cases, requests by IRS for current control information were denied mainly because of non-disclosure requirements claimed by the owners of the external systems. The guidance also specifies that in addition to these procedures, user entities should obtain an annual assurance statement from their service providers' management that highlights the key controls and the results of annual testing, the objectives of which should be aligned with the user entity's annual assessment. However, IRS did not obtain assurance statements from its service providers but rather relied on them to inform it if there were any significant changes or security issues affecting the system. Consequently, for many of the external systems that support its financial reporting, IRS did not have sufficient, appropriate evidence that internal control was effective as of September 30, 2013. IRS has implemented internal controls over the transactions affected by these external systems that help to reduce the risk of undetected misstatements. However, the lack of sufficient, appropriate evidence that internal control at these service providers was effective hinders IRS's ability to ensure that its financial data is secure.

During this year's audit, we also found new deficiencies in internal control over IRS's financial reporting systems. For example, IRS (1) allowed individuals to make changes to mainframe processing without following its established change control procedures to ensure changes were authorized; (2) did not include sufficient detail in its authorization process to ensure that access to systems was appropriate; and (3) did not configure certain applications to use strong encryption for authentication, increasing the potential for unauthorized access.

---

[19]According to IRS, of the nine financial systems it identified as external, the U.S. Department of Agriculture's National Finance Center (NFC) is the service provider for two of the financial systems, the Department of the Treasury is the service provider for five of the financial systems, and the General Services Administration and the U.S. Postal Service each acted as the service provider for one financial system. NFC is IRS's only service provider that obtains an annual report on the effectiveness of its internal control upon which other entities, such as IRS, can rely to support significant aspects of their operations. This report on NFC's internal control is conducted by a service auditor pursuant to Statement on Standards for Attestation Engagements No. 16, *Reporting on Controls at a Service Organization*.

Although IRS has a comprehensive framework for its information security program, some aspects of it have not yet been effectively implemented. For example, IRS's testing methodology did not always determine whether required controls were operating effectively; consequently, we continued to identify control weaknesses that had not been detected by IRS. Further, IRS had not updated key mainframe policies and procedures to address issues such as users accessing files used by one processing environment from a different environment, thereby increasing the risk of unauthorized or erroneous changes to tax processing systems.

In light of the control risks created by IRS's ongoing information security deficiencies, continued and consistent management commitment and attention to an effective information security program will be essential to the maintenance of, and continued improvements in, its information system controls. Until IRS takes additional steps to (1) more effectively implement its testing and monitoring capabilities, (2) ensure that policies and procedures are updated, and (3) address unresolved and newly identified control deficiencies, its financial and taxpayer data will remain vulnerable to inappropriate and undetected use, modification, or disclosure.

## Other Matters

### Required Supplementary Information

U.S. generally accepted accounting principles issued by the Federal Accounting Standards Advisory Board (FASAB) require that the RSI be presented to supplement the financial statements. Although not a part of the financial statements, FASAB considers this information to be an essential part of financial reporting for placing the financial statements in appropriate operational, economic, or historical context. We have applied certain limited procedures to the RSI in accordance with U.S. generally accepted government auditing standards, which consisted of inquiries of management about the methods of preparing the RSI and comparing the information for consistency with management's responses to the auditor's inquiries, the financial statements, and other knowledge we obtained during the audit of the financial statements, in order to report omissions or material departures from FASAB guidelines, if any, identified by these limited procedures. We did not audit and we do not express an opinion or provide any assurance on the RSI because the limited procedures we applied do not provide sufficient evidence to express an opinion or provide any assurance.

| Other Information | IRS's other information contains a wide range of information, some of which is not directly related to the financial statements. This information is presented for purposes of additional analysis and is not a required part of the financial statements or the RSI. We read the other information included with the financial statements in order to identify material inconsistencies, if any, with the audited financial statements. Our audit was conducted for the purpose of forming an opinion on IRS's financial statements. We did not audit and do not express an opinion or provide any assurance on the other information. |
|---|---|
| Other Financial Management Challenges | In addition to the challenge of addressing its internal control deficiencies, IRS also faces other significant financial management challenges related to (1) the safeguarding of taxpayer receipts and associated information and (2) significant improper refunds from identity theft. |

### Safeguarding Taxpayer Receipts and Associated Information

IRS faces an ongoing management challenge because of the millions of hard copy tax returns along with hundreds of billions of dollars in associated taxpayer payments it receives and processes each year. As long as IRS continues to receive large volumes of hard copy taxpayer payments and supporting data, there will continue to be a significant risk to the government and taxpayers alike that loss of receipts or inappropriate disclosure or compromise of taxpayer information may occur during this process. Safeguarding these taxpayer receipts and associated taxpayer information to prevent such events is among IRS's most important and demanding responsibilities. Congressional and taxpayer expectations in this regard are justifiably high. During our financial audits of IRS, including this year's audit, we continued to identify deficiencies in IRS's internal control intended to safeguard taxpayer receipts and information that while not individually or in the aggregate constituting a significant deficiency or material weakness, are nonetheless sensitive matters requiring IRS management's attention. We have made numerous recommendations to address these issues, to which IRS has been responsive.[20] Nonetheless, it is critical that IRS continue to maintain effective internal control necessary to appropriately

---

[20]We have reported these deficiencies and recommendations to address them, as well as IRS's associated corrective actions, in various management and status of recommendations reports to IRS. See, for example, GAO-13-420R.

mitigate this risk, including ongoing monitoring of key internal controls to ensure that they do not deteriorate over time.

## Preventing and Detecting Improper Refunds from Identity Theft

Identity theft-related tax fraud is a hardship for its victims and a growing problem for tax administration. IRS management continues to face a significant challenge arising from the large numbers of identity theft-based refund claims it receives. This form of identity theft occurs when an individual uses a stolen taxpayer's name and taxpayer identification number[21] (generally a Social Security number) to file fraudulent tax returns claiming tax refunds. Fraudulent refund claims are often submitted to IRS early in the filing season, before the victims, whose identities have been stolen, file their tax returns. In many such cases, the fraudulent refund claim is only discovered after the legitimate taxpayer files his or her tax return and IRS realizes that a refund has already been paid on the taxpayer's account. The legitimate taxpayer's refund is delayed while IRS spends time determining which claim is legitimate, thus causing an undue burden for the victim of the identity theft.

IRS is aware of the growing magnitude of identity theft-based fraudulent refund claims and has devoted significant resources to addressing the problem. According to IRS, it identified and prevented the payment of over 1.8 million identity theft-based refund claims totaling over $12.1 billion in calendar year 2012, and over 1.4 million such claims totaling over $8.4 billion in the first 9 months of calendar year 2013. However, the number of identity theft-based refund claims IRS did not identify or stop during this period and their associated cost to the federal government is unknown. IRS has developed a strategy to address identity theft, including efforts to prevent and detect identity theft-based refund claims.[22] According to IRS, this strategy serves as the foundation of its efforts to reduce the effects of identity theft. For example, IRS has (1) continually enhanced its various internal tools designed to screen refund claims and stop those with characteristics of identity theft for

---

[21]A taxpayer identification number is a number assigned to taxpayers for identification purposes. Depending on the type of the taxpayer, this can be a Social Security number, an Employer Identification Number, or an Individual Taxpayer Identification Number assigned to individuals who are not eligible to obtain Social Security numbers.

[22]GAO, *Taxes and Identity Theft: Status of IRS Initiatives to Help Victimized Taxpayers*, GAO-11-721T (Washington, D.C.: June 2, 2011).

further investigation, (2) provided taxpayers with targeted information to increase their awareness of the threat, and (3) offered personal identification numbers to past victims to help them prevent a recurrence.

However, the options available to IRS in attempting to minimize identity theft-related refund claims are affected by a number of constraints.[23] For example, (1) the personal information contained in tax returns and related information submitted to IRS is confidential and is protected from disclosure except as specifically authorized by statute, which places limitations on IRS's ability to share it with other entities affected by identity theft, including law enforcement agencies;[24] (2) IRS cannot match third-party information returns with tax returns before refunds are issued; and (3) the benefits to be derived by more rigorous screening for potentially fraudulent tax returns must be weighed against the adverse effects of increased taxpayer burden as the increased scrutiny inevitably delays payment of valid refunds to legitimate taxpayers. Moreover, because the full magnitude of identity theft-related refund fraud continues to be unknown, the effectiveness of IRS's efforts is unclear.

If IRS is to minimize the effects of identity theft-based refund claims on taxpayers and the federal government, it is critical for IRS to continue to explore all options available in order to effectively identify, design, and implement the most appropriate measures to prevent and detect identity theft-related refund fraud.

# Report on Compliance with Laws, Regulations, Contracts, and Grant Agreements

In connection with our audits of IRS's financial statements, we have tested compliance with selected provisions of applicable laws, regulations, contracts, and grant agreements consistent with our auditor's responsibility discussed below. We caution that noncompliance may occur and not be detected by these tests. We performed our tests of compliance in accordance with U.S. generally accepted government auditing standards.

---

[23]GAO-11-721T.

[24]26 U.S.C. § 6103.

| Management's Responsibility | IRS management is responsible for complying with laws, regulations, contracts, and grant agreements applicable to IRS. |
|---|---|
| Auditor's Responsibility | Our responsibility is to test compliance with selected provisions of laws, regulations, contracts, and grant agreements applicable to IRS that have a direct effect on the determination of material amounts and disclosures in the IRS financial statements, and perform certain other limited procedures. Accordingly, we did not test compliance with all laws, regulations, contracts, and grant agreements applicable to IRS. |
| Results of Our Tests for Compliance with Laws, Regulations, Contracts, and Grant Agreements | Our tests for compliance with selected provisions of applicable laws, regulations, contracts, and grant agreements disclosed no instances of noncompliance for fiscal year 2013 that would be reportable under U.S. generally accepted government auditing standards. However, the objective of our tests was not to provide an opinion on overall compliance with laws, regulations, contracts, and grant agreements applicable to IRS. Accordingly, we do not express such an opinion. |
| Intended Purpose of Report on Compliance with Laws, Regulations, Contracts, and Grant Agreements | The purpose of this report is solely to describe the scope of our testing of compliance with selected provisions of applicable laws, regulations, contracts, and grant agreements and the results of that testing, and not to provide an opinion on compliance. This report is an integral part of an audit performed in accordance with U.S. generally accepted government auditing standards in considering compliance. Accordingly, this report on compliance with laws, regulations, contracts, and grant agreements is not suitable for any other purpose. |
| Agency Comments | In commenting on a draft of this report, IRS stated that it was pleased that we recognized its progress in strengthening controls over information security. IRS also stated that while challenges remain, it has a solid management team dedicated to promoting the highest standard of financial management, and would continue to increase the focus on information security and internal controls while improving financial reporting. |

We will evaluate the effectiveness of IRS's corrective actions during our audit of IRS's fiscal year 2014 financial statements. The complete text of IRS's response is reprinted in appendix II.

*Cheryl E. Clark*

Cheryl E. Clark
Director
Financial Management and Assurance

December 11, 2013

## *Internal Revenue Service*

Management's Discussion and Analysis
Fiscal Year 2013

"Taxes are what we pay for a civilized society."
Oliver Wendell Holmes, Jr., U.S. Supreme Court Justice

INTERNAL REVENUE SERVICE
Management's Discussion & Analysis
Fiscal Year 2013

# IRS VISION, MISSION, AND ORGANIZATION

## Vision

Funding America's future by strengthening our system of voluntary tax compliance.

## Mission

Provide America's taxpayers top-quality service by helping them understand and meet their tax responsibilities and enforce the law with integrity and fairness to all.

## History

The IRS is one of the oldest bureaus in the United States Government. Article 1, Section 8 of the Constitution gave the Federal Government the power to "lay and collect Taxes, Duties, Imposts and Excises, to pay the Debts and provide for the common Defence and general Welfare of the United States…" In 1862, President Lincoln and the Congress established the Bureau of Internal Revenue and the nation's first income tax. In 1953, the Bureau of Internal Revenue's name was changed to the Internal Revenue Service (IRS).

## Strategic Goals

The IRS Strategic Plan guides the IRS in its work by emphasizing these two overarching goals and its strategic foundations:

*Goal 1:* Improve service to make voluntary compliance easier
*Goal 2:* Enforce the law to ensure everyone meets their obligation to pay taxes
*Strategic Foundations:* Invest for high performance

## Employees

In FY 2013, the IRS employed approximately 98,000 people, including over 20,000 temporary and seasonal staff.

## Location

The IRS headquarters is located at 1111 Constitution Ave., NW, Washington, DC 20224. There are also over 600 offices in all states and territories and some U.S. embassies and consulates.

## Internet

The IRS provides tax information, taxpayer services, forms, and publications at www.IRS.gov.

1

INTERNAL REVENUE SERVICE
Management's Discussion & Analysis
Fiscal Year 2013

## Organization Structure and Accountability

The IRS has three commissioner-level organizations.

| Commissioner, Internal Revenue Service | Deputy Commissioner for Services and Enforcement | Deputy Commissioner for Operations Support |
|---|---|---|
| *(Specialized IRS units report directly to the Commissioner's Office)* | *(Reports directly to the Commissioner and oversees the four primary operating divisions and other service and enforcement functions)* | *(Reports directly to the Commissioner and oversees the IRS support functions, facilitating economy of scale efficiencies and better business practices)* |
| • Chief Counsel <br> • Appeals <br> • Taxpayer Advocate Service <br> • Equity, Diversity and Inclusion <br> • Research, Analysis, and Statistics <br> • Communications and Liaison <br> • Office of Compliance Analytics | • Wage and Investment Division <br> • Large Business and International Division <br> • Small Business/Self Employed Division <br> • Tax Exempt and Government Entities Division <br> • Criminal Investigation <br> • Office of Professional Responsibility <br> • Affordable Care Act Office <br> • Office of Online Services <br> • Return Preparer Office <br> • Whistleblower Office | • Information Technology <br> • Agency-Wide Shared Services <br> • Privacy, Government Liaison and Disclosure <br> • Human Capital Office <br> • Chief Financial Office |

## Tax Statistics Highlights

| FY 2013 Tax Stats at a Glance | |
|---|---|
| Total Returns Processed | 241 million |
| Total Revenue Collected | $2.9 trillion |
| Enforcement Revenue Collected | $53.3 billion |
| Total Refunds | $364 billion |
| Avg. Individual Refund | $2,646 |
| E-File Rate - Individual | 82.5% |
| E-File Rate - Business | 40.2% |
| IRS.gov Page Views | 1.9 billion |
| "Where's My Refund?" Usage | 192.3 million |
| Number of Downloads from IRS.gov | 217.5 million |

2

INTERNAL REVENUE SERVICE
Management's Discussion & Analysis
Fiscal Year 2013

# FINANCIAL RESOURCES

The IRS FY 2013 post sequestration operating level was $11.2 billion, a decrease of more than $600 million below FY 2012. In addition to the appropriated budget, IRS funding also included $731 million from user fees, reimbursable, and unobligated balances from prior years for a total operating level of $12 billion.

**Funding by Appropriations ($ thousands)**

**Taxpayer Services** *[$2,135,553]* funds processing tax returns and related documents, and assistance for taxpayers in filing returns and paying taxes due.

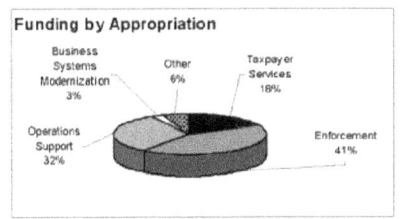

Funding by Appropriation

**Enforcement** *[$4,949,178]* funds examination of tax returns, collection of balances, the administrative and judicial settlement of taxpayer appeals of examination findings, as well as providing resources for strengthened enforcement to reduce invalid claims and erroneous filings associated with the Earned Income Tax Credit (EITC) program.

**Operations Support** *[$3,800,943]* funds administrative services, policy management and IRS-wide support. The appropriation also funds staffing, equipment, and related costs to manage, maintain, and operate critical information systems that support tax administration.

**Business Systems Modernization** *[$312,938]* funds capital asset acquisitions of information technology systems to modernize key tax administration systems.

In addition to the core appropriations, the IRS has the following appropriations (special funds):

**User Fees** *[$353,010]* from payment for services provided, **Reimbursable Resources** *[$94,392]*, and **Unobligated Balances** *[$283,892]* from prior years' transfers in/out.

## Use of Resources

Funding levels reflect the approved transfer of up to $73M from Enforcement to Taxpayer Services and Operations Support accounts. These transfers were required to mitigate the impact of sequestration and to ensure furloughs were equitably managed.

The IRS uses a cost allocation methodology to assign support and overhead costs to each program described below. The Statement of Net Cost reflects the use of IRS resources in conducting its major programs and reports the full cost of these programs in accordance with the Statement of Federal Financial Accounting Standards No. 4, "Managerial Cost Accounting."

- **Taxpayer Assistance and Education** activities *[5%]* include taxpayer education and outreach, tax publication issuance and distribution.

3

INTERNAL REVENUE SERVICE
Management's Discussion & Analysis
Fiscal Year 2013

- **Filing and Account Services** activities *[30%]* include filing tax returns, maintaining customer accounts, and processing taxpayer information.

### How IRS Uses Its Resources

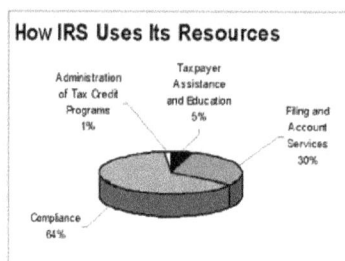

| Use of Resources ($) | | |
|---|---|---|
| Program | FY 2013 | FY 2012 |
| **Taxpayer Assistance and Education** | $607,408 | $925,137 |
| **Filing and Account Services** | $3,828,546 | $3,571,572 |
| **Compliance** | $8,196,759 | $8,571,093 |
| **Administration of Tax Credit Programs** | $168,989 | $180,020 |

- **Compliance** activities *[64%]* include pre-filing agreements, document matching, examination, collection, and criminal investigation activities.

- **Administration of Tax Credit Programs'** *[1%]* primarily includes costs for Earned Income Tax Credit (EITC) program activities.

## PERFORMANCE SUMMARY

Since FY 2010, the IRS received reductions to appropriated funding totaling almost $1 billion. In FY 2011 and FY 2012, the IRS budget allocation decreased by 0.2% and 2.5%, respectively. In FY 2013, sequestration and a rescission combined to reduce the IRS FY 2012 budget by $618 million. This resulted in the IRS re-evaluating operating levels to ensure critical programs continued to be delivered. During FY 2013, the IRS collected $2.9 trillion, using a budget of $11.2 billion, accounting for 91% of the total revenue that the U.S. government received. This substantial return on investment provides the funds that allow our government to operate.

Total Enforcement Revenue Collected increased $3.2 billion over FY 2012. Of this amount, $2.6 billion is attributed to a small number of cases that came in while in an appeals or litigation status pertaining to cases worked in prior years, which accounted for 79% of the enforcement revenue growth.

### IRS Enforcement Revenue ($ Billions)

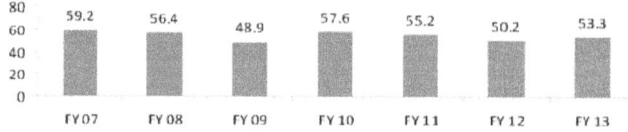

' Prior to fiscal year 2012, this program also included the costs of administering the health coverage tax credit (HCTC). Those costs are now included under Filing and Account Services activities, except for costs related to HCTC obligations made prior to FY 2012, which remain here.

4

INTERNAL REVENUE SERVICE
Management's Discussion & Analysis
Fiscal Year 2013

The IRS National Research Program (NRP) analyzes reporting compliance data for various taxpayer populations, including Individual Income Tax, Corporate Income Tax, Employment Taxes, and Fuel Excise Taxes. NRP results enhance taxpayer service by improving IRS processes to reduce taxpayer burden and support enforcement activities by identifying issues with high risks for noncompliance. The IRS Joint Statistical Research Program (JSRP) uses Statistics of Income tax data, to study the effects of existing tax policies on individuals, businesses, and the economy. The JSRP included 20 projects collaborating with academia, non-profit research organizations, and other government agencies on important issues affecting tax administration. In FY 2013, the JSRP developed an IRS Databank, which provides a new way of looking at tax return data at the individual level rather than the return level. This key difference will facilitate better understanding of the impact of taxes on individuals.

# PERFORMANCE GOALS, OBJECTIVES, AND RESULTS

The IRS strives to deliver a high level of performance both in taxpayer service and enforcement of the tax laws to ensure everyone meets their obligation to pay taxes. These goals are supported by investing in two strategic foundations – our people and our technology.

## GOAL 1: Improve Service to Make Voluntary Compliance Easier

Providing taxpayers top-quality service and helping them understand and meet their tax obligations remained top priorities for the IRS.

By assisting taxpayers with their tax questions before they filed their returns, the IRS helped prevent inadvertent noncompliance and reduced burdensome post-filing notices and other correspondence from the IRS. Accordingly, the IRS provided year-round assistance to millions of taxpayers through many sources, including outreach and education programs, issuance of tax forms and publications, rulings and regulations, toll-free call centers, IRS.gov, Taxpayer Assistance Centers (TAC), Volunteer Income Tax Assistance (VITA) and Tax Counseling for the Elderly (TCE) sites.

During FY 2013, the IRS updated forms to help taxpayers comply with filing requirements, converting forms for visually impaired taxpayers and translating more tax products into multiple languages. In addition, the IRS continued its effort to redesign taxpayer correspondence in plain language and in a consistent format to make it easier for taxpayers to understand their obligations. The IRS released 56 redesigned notices; bringing the total in production to 181.

### Highlights of the 2013 Filing Season

The IRS delivered another successful filing season in 2013, rising to the challenges posed by tax legislation enacted on January 2, 2013. Despite the late legislation, the IRS took the necessary steps to minimize disruptions for taxpayers. The filing season began on January 30, 2013, less than one month after the passage the legislation that affected over 600 tax products. Results of the 2013 filing-season included:

- Processing over 147.6 million individual returns and issuing 118.7 million refunds totaling almost $314 billion compared to 121.6 million refunds totaling $333 billion for the same period in 2012.

5

INTERNAL REVENUE SERVICE
Management's Discussion & Analysis
Fiscal Year 2013

- Achieving a 60.5% telephone level of service.
- Answering 30.1 million assistor calls, a 2.2% increase from 2012.
- Answering 54.0 million automated calls.
- Responding correctly to 95.7% of tax law questions and 96.0% of account questions received via the telephone.
- Processing 49,202 Savings Bond requests, totaling $21.8 million.

Growth in taxpayer satisfaction has been steady and strong over the last several years, as the 2012 overall score is seven percentage points higher than the 68 reached in 2008. According to the latest American Customer Satisfaction Index Survey, taxpayer satisfaction with the tax filing experience in 2012 reached a score of 75 on a scale of 100, 6.6 points higher than the Federal Government aggregate of 68.4, and the highest score the IRS received since the survey began in 1994.

Taxpayer Service Facts

- Served over 6.5 million taxpayers at 390 Taxpayer Assistance Center (TAC) offices throughout the country.
- Assisted over 81,000 customers through Facilitated Self-Assistance (FSA) kiosks.
- Assisted over 1,300 taxpayers who were victims of Super Storm Sandy by extending hours in 11 TAC offices and holding an open house at six TACs.
- Issued 62 filing season Tax Tips, 15 Special Edition Tax Tips, and 26 Summertime Tax Tips, which reached nearly 465,000 subscribers.
- Translated 50 Tax Tips into Spanish.

The IRS continued to support traditional services from its national walk-in sites while meeting increased taxpayer demand for technology-driven services including expansion of the Virtual Service Delivery (VSD) project and e-file opportunities.

The VSD project allowed taxpayers to have face-to-face interactions with IRS assistors working in remote locations using video monitors. This year, the IRS collaborated with internal and external stakeholders to deploy VSD systems in 14 new locations bringing the total to 26 sites and assisted over 22,000 taxpayers with accounts, tax law questions, and other inquiries.

Individual and business electronically-filed (e-file) returns continued to grow. Quicker refunds and a more efficient way for taxpayers to file accurate returns, coupled with innovative technology, such as home computer filing, contributed to the increase in e-file returns. FY 2013 e-file results included:

- Individual returns electronically filed increased to 82.5%, up from 80.5% in 2012, totaling 121.9 million electronically filed returns.
- Home-Computer filing increased to 45.2 million returns, up from 43.5 million in 2012, a 3.9% increase.
- Business returns were filed electronically at a rate of 40.2%, up from 36.7% in 2012, due to increases in the e-file rate of employers' quarterly and annual wage reporting and exempt organizations returns.
- Tax professional use of e-file increased 1.5% from the previous year, reaching 76.7 million returns.

6

The IRS enhanced existing online and self-help service options by increasing the amount of tax information and services available to taxpayers through IRS.gov. Self-service applications on IRS.gov enabled taxpayers to exchange information online with the IRS, decreasing service requests from higher-cost channels like telephone assistance.

IRS.gov continued to be the primary method for providing tax information and services to taxpayers. In FY 2013, taxpayers viewed IRS.gov web pages more than 1.87 billion times, using the website to:

- Get forms and publications. More than 217.5 million tax products were downloaded.
- Link to the Electronic Federal Tax Payment System (EFTPS). EFTPS processed more than 145 million electronic tax payments totaling $2.3 trillion.
- Get answers. More than 2.4 million visits to the Interactive Tax Assistant introduction page where taxpayers can receive answers to tax law questions.
- Check on refunds. Taxpayers used "Where's My Refund?" more than 200.5 million times to check on the status of their tax refunds, an increase of 51.6% from 2012.

In FY 2013, the IRS enhanced the "Where's My Refund?" web tool to allow taxpayers to find out when their tax return was received, when the refund was approved, and when the refund was sent. These enhancements reduced the time taxpayers had to wait to get a status of their tax returns from 72 hours to 24 hours. The IRS notified taxpayers of the enhanced "Where's My Refund?" web tool by placing questions and answers on IRS.gov and producing two YouTube videos, "When Will I Get My Refund?" which had over 1.1 million views and "How to Use the Where's My Refund? " tool, which had over 211,000 views.

The IRS also deployed a new telephone and web tool called *"Where's My Amended Return?"* in both English and Spanish that allowed taxpayers to check the status of their Form 1040X amended tax returns for the current year and up to three prior years. The tool also provided taxpayers with information such as when their amended return was received, adjusted, and completed, as well as specific information regarding offset conditions such as a previous IRS tax liability or a past due obligation.

Taxpayer Education and Outreach

The IRS continued to improve and expand on its outreach and educational services through partnerships with state taxing authorities, volunteer groups, social media, webinars, and other methods to address taxpayer needs.

Each year, the IRS and its partners provide free tax assistance to the elderly, disabled, and limited English proficient individuals and families at VITA and TCE sites. In FY 2013, more than 91,800 volunteers prepared over 3.4 million federal returns, 95.3% of which were filed electronically, and over 2.5 million state returns. In addition, the IRS teamed up with its national partners to offer a remote filing method – Facilitated Self Assistance (FSA) at VITA sites. More than 82,000 FSA returns were filed at the 330 VITA sites offering the FSA remote filing model. Taxpayers with incomes of $57,000 or less, basic computer skills, internet access with an e-mail address, and necessary tax preparation documents could file their taxes using this model.

The Earned Income Tax Credit (EITC) is one of the federal government's largest benefit programs for low-income working families and individuals. In FY 2013, the IRS held its seventh annual EITC Awareness Day, promoting EITC awareness and free return preparation options. Through 658 outreach activities, including news conferences, news releases, newsletters, e-

7

mails, and an increased use of social media tools, the IRS achieved nationwide coverage in both English and Spanish markets, including over 15,000 hits on IRS.gov.

In addition to proving effective in reaching EITC taxpayers, social media tools provided all taxpayers and stakeholders increased access to IRS messages. In FY 2013, the IRS shared information on the following social media platforms:

- IRS2Go V3 — In February 2013, the IRS launched a new version of the IRS2Go smartphone application, which lets taxpayers interact with the IRS using their Internetwork Operating System (IOS) and Android devices. Over 2.5 million users downloaded the IRS2Go application in FY 2013. The new version provided the application in Spanish for the first time and included minor updates to the existing functionality. IRS2Go V3 now provides the following functionality:

    o Get Your Refund Status - Users can check the status of their federal refund.
    o Get My Tax Record - Users can order their tax account or tax return transcript.
    o Watch Us - Users can view the IRS YouTube videos right on their smartphones in English, Spanish and American Sign Language.
    o Follow the IRS - Users can sign up to follow the IRS Twitter newsfeeds.
    o Get Tax Updates - Users enter their e-mail address to get tips and reminders to help with tax planning and preparation.
    o Get the Latest News - Users can quickly access the most recent updates on the IRS.gov English and Spanish news pages.

- Tumblr - In FY 2013, the IRS added Tumblr to its list of social media platforms to share IRS news and information. Tumblr is a micro-blogging platform where users can access and share text, photos, and videos from their browser, smartphone, tablet, or desktop. The new Tumblr account at http://internalrevenueservice.tumblr.com, provided taxpayers another way to get tax information by accessing helpful tips, videos, podcasts and more, and made it easier for IRS partners and others to share tax information they received from the IRS. In FY 2013, the IRS created and posted 197 blog entries, which were viewed almost 215,000 times.

- YouTube - Viewers can watch IRS channels for short, informative videos in English, Spanish, American Sign Language and other languages. The IRS created 35 new videos for the 2013 filing season, bringing the total to more than 130 videos, with more than 3.2 million views.

- Twitter - Taxpayers can get announcements and information using five corporate IRS Twitter accounts. Tax-related announcements are available at @IRSnews and @IRSenEspanol, @IRStaxpros covers news for tax professionals, and @RecruitmentIRS provides updates for job seekers about hiring initiatives. The Taxpayer Advocate Service has information available at @YourVoiceAtIRS. More than 82,000 people followed the IRS Twitter feeds, an increase of over 35%. In FY 2013, the IRS pushed out nearly 6,800 messages, an average of over 18 tweets per day. Messages included news releases, tax tips, links to YouTube videos and Tumblr posts, refund/return issues, and many useful links to IRS information; which were re-tweeted and pushed out to hundreds of thousands of Twitter users.

8

INTERNAL REVENUE SERVICE
Management's Discussion & Analysis
Fiscal Year 2013

- iTunes - Taxpayers can download audio files for use in podcasts that explain important tax information.

- IRS Facebook - taxpayers can get tax information and links to IRS.gov regarding hot topics.

- IRS Return Preparer Office Facebook – The IRS engages with the return preparer audience to share relevant tax information.

- Linkedin – The IRS uses this business professional social network to reach professional tax return preparers and easily share information about the oversight program, exchange ideas and promote best practices, all in an effort to improve tax administration.

The IRS also expanded the Customer Early Warning System (CEWS) to include toll-free calls and taxpayer correspondence programs. Using Customer Service Representative Feedback, contact analytics, walk-in operations, social media monitoring, and external partners, such as VITA sites, the IRS was able to detect emerging issues that affected the taxpayer experience. In FY 2013, the CEWS identified developing issues involving e-File, Identity Theft Protection Personal Identification Number (IP PIN), the processing of certain forms, and "Where's My Refund?" Early detection of these issues allowed the IRS to promptly address them and eliminate confusion and reduce burden for millions of taxpayers.

In FY 2013, the IRS also provided tax information in a webinar format, which proved to be a popular, meaningful, and cost-effective educational and outreach tool for the tax professional community and Stakeholder Liaison (SL) personnel. The IRS rebroadcasted a webinar titled, "Circular 230 Overview: Key Provisions & Responsibilities for Tax Professionals," four times. The webinar included a live 20-minute Q&A session and was viewed by approximately 6,500 tax professionals and over 17,600 times since its original broadcast. In FY 2013, the IRS reached over 55,700 tax professionals and IRS employees during 121 events, including in-person, telephonic and electronic media.

The IRS assisted individual taxpayers facing financial hardship due to the struggling economy including those who filed for bankruptcy or owed IRS past due amounts by:

- Creating and publishing new Publication 5082 titled, "*What You Should Know About Chapter 13 Bankruptcy and Delinquent Tax Returns*." This publication provided answers to several common Chapter 13 filer questions and addressed filing and payment topics.

- Deploying a new tool on IRS.gov called, "*Offer in Compromise Pre-Qualifier*," which required the taxpayer to answer a few simple questions and enter basic financial information to determine if they were a candidate for an Offer in Compromise (OIC). An OIC allows a taxpayer to settle a tax debt for less than the full amount owed.

**Strategic Goal 1 Performance Measures**

While IRS was not able to achieve all of its targets, the accuracy or quality of our results were not impacted by the drastic reductions to funding.

9

INTERNAL REVENUE SERVICE
Management's Discussion & Analysis
Fiscal Year 2013

The IRS met or exceeded 67% (8 of 12) of its Taxpayer Service performance targets in FY 2013.

**Strategic Goal 1: Improve Service to Make Voluntary Compliance Easier**

| | FY 2013 | |
|---|---|---|
| | Target | Actual |
| Customer Service Representative (CSR) Level of Service | 70.0% | 60.5% |
| Customer Contacts Resolved per Staff Year | 16,754 | 20,767 |
| Customer Accuracy – Tax Law Phones | 93.0% | 95.7% |
| Customer Accuracy – Customer Accounts (Phones) | 95.0% | 96.0% |
| Timeliness of Critical Filing Season Tax Products to the Public | 95.0% | 58.9% |
| Timeliness of Critical TE/GE and Business Tax Products to the Public | 95.0% | 83.6% |
| Percent Individual Returns Processed Electronically | 80.0% | 82.5% |
| Cost per Taxpayer Served ($) (HCTC) | $15.00 | $13.41 |
| Sign-Up Time (Days) – Customer Engagement (HCTC) | 125.0 | 125.2 |
| Percent Business Returns Processed Electronically | 38.0% | 40.2% |
| Refund Timeliness – Individual (Paper) | 98.0% | 99.0% |
| Taxpayer Self Assistance Rate | 80.0% | 83.3% |

**Shortfall Explanations** – The impact of late legislation enacted in January 2013 and the effects of sequestration were significant impediments to the ability of the IRS to achieve all taxpayer service goals. IRS funding for taxpayer service was decreased over $100 million in FY 2013 from FY 2012 as a result of sequestration.

**CSR Level of Service (LOS):** The Customer Service Representative (CSR) Level of Service (LOS) target for FY 2013 (70%) was established prior to the notice of sequestration. When the sequester cuts took effect, the required funding adjustment severely hampered the IRS's ability to meet the original target. In addition, demand for toll-free service increased over last year by almost 10 percent, which further strained reduced resources.

**Timeliness of Critical Filing Season Tax Products to the Public:** The late-passage of the American Taxpayer Relief Act of 2012 (enacted on January 2) negatively impacted the ability to deliver timely critical tax products.

**Timeliness of Critical TE/GE and Business Tax Products to the Public:** The late-passage of the American Taxpayer Relief Act of 2012 (enacted on January 2) negatively impacted our ability to deliver timely critical tax products.

**Sign-Up Time (Days) – Customer Engagement (HCTC):** HCTC continued to average 15 days from receipt of registration to enrollment. Sign-up time is measured from when the taxpayers are notified of their eligibility to until they choose to register for the credit and is therefore, out of IRS control.

## GOAL 2: Enforce the law to ensure everyone meets their obligation to pay taxes

Enforcing the tax laws is an integral component of IRS efforts to enhance voluntary compliance. IRS enforcement activities, such as examination and collection, remained a high priority. In

10

INTERNAL REVENUE SERVICE
Management's Discussion & Analysis
Fiscal Year 2013

FY 2013, the IRS increased its efforts to confront refund fraud caused by identity theft; enhanced issue resolution programs to reduce uncertainty around tax positions; focused on international tax evasion; and better leveraged the tax return preparer community.

**Highlights of Enforcement Performance**

The IRS places mission-critical importance on enforcement of the tax law, especially as tax administration becomes increasingly complex. This importance is demonstrated both by the portion of our budget dedicated to enforcement activities, 41% in FY 2013, and by our diligent efforts to ensure we are maximizing the productivity of those expenditures. As a result of the impacts of sequestration and furloughs, IRS delivered key enforcement programs at levels below 2012.

- High income audits: 172,128.
- Small business audits (assets <$10 million): 51,594.
- Large corporate audits: 14,547.
- Individual audits: 1.4 million.

**Enforcement Facts**

- Completed over 4.1 million automated underreporter contact closures.
- Closed over 2.9 million collection cases.
- Completed 48,892 tax-exempt and government entities compliance contacts.
- Collected over $601 million through the Federal Payment Levy Program.
- Collected over $192 million from taxpayers who owe a federal tax debt through the State Income Tax Levy Program.

In FY 2013, the IRS enhanced issue resolution programs to reduce uncertainty, mitigate administrative tax risk for individual and large corporate taxpayers, and increase organizational efficiency. The IRS issue resolution programs include:

- International Joint Audit Initiative. An initiative where two or more jurisdictions combine to form a single audit team to conduct simultaneous examinations that involve the U.S. and one or more of its tax treaty partners. The team audits the issues/transactions of a jointly selected taxpayer, instead of conducting independent audits. In FY 2013, the IRS led and coordinated 4 joint audits and sought additional opportunities to expand the joint audit process to additional taxpayers and U.S. treaty partners.

- Compliance Assurance Process (CAP) Program. A program that allows large corporate taxpayers to resolve tax issues prior to filing a tax return. CAP consists of three distinct components:

    o Pre-CAP – Provides interested taxpayers with clear direction on how to gain entry into CAP. In FY 2013, 26 corporations participated in Pre-CAP.

    o CAP - 169 corporate taxpayers participated in CAP, with 153 of them returning from the previous year.

11

INTERNAL REVENUE SERVICE
Management's Discussion & Analysis
Fiscal Year 2013

- o CAP Maintenance – Allows taxpayers who have been in CAP, have few complex issues, and have established a track record of working cooperatively to receive a reduced level of IRS review. The program had 44 participants in 2013.

- Industry Issue Resolution (IIR) program. The IIR program identifies frequently disputed or burdensome tax issues that are common to a significant number of business taxpayers and may be resolved through published or other administrative guidance. Since program initiation, 159 IIRs have been submitted, with 41 accepted. In FY 2013, one submission was rejected, one was accepted, and five are in process.

- Fast Track Settlement (FTS) program. FTS allows taxpayers to settle issues with an Appeals officer during the audit process instead of after the audit. In FY 2013, the FTS program was expanded nationally for Small Business Self-Employed taxpayers. Cycle time and average hours spent on a case decreased by 267 days and six hours, respectively.

- Uncertain Tax Positions (UTP) program. UTP aims at having transparent discussions with corporations to resolve issues much quicker and increase efficiency by targeting taxpayers and issues with the highest risk of non-compliance. In FY 2013, 2,138 taxpayers filed Schedule UTP for Tax Year 2011 of which 42% of the schedules included only one uncertain tax position.

- Voluntary Classification Settlement Program (VCSP). VCSP increased tax compliance and reduced burden by providing greater certainty for employers, workers, and the government. In FY 2013, VCSP was expanded to pave the way for more taxpayers to take advantage of this low-cost option for achieving certainty under the law by reclassifying their workers as employees for future tax periods. Since implementation in October 2011, 1,357 employers have applied to the VCSP program covering 24,554 workers, with $3.2 million in settlement payments.

The IRS strategic enforcement efforts and parallel Offshore Voluntary Disclosure Program (OVDP) gave U.S. taxpayers with undisclosed offshore assets or income an opportunity to become compliant with the U.S. tax system and avoid potential criminal charges. The OVDP program has resulted in the collection of more than $5.5 billion in back taxes, interest, and penalties from approximately 38,000 participants since the program reopened in January 2012.

International compliance programs have provided the IRS with a wealth of information on various banks and advisors assisting people with offshore tax evasion, which the IRS is using to continue its international enforcement efforts. In FY 2013, the IRS continued to implement strategies to address international issues by improving intra-governmental coordination, expanding IRS presence in U.S. territories, and enhancing compliance measures using customer-tailored strategies. The following actions were completed in FY 2013:

- Foreign Account Tax Compliance Act (FATCA). The IRS continued to lead the design and implementation of the Foreign Financial Institution registration and intergovernmental data exchange processes by working with foreign governments to develop a network of Intergovernmental Agreements.

12

- Report of Foreign Bank and Financial Accounts (FBAR) Communications. The IRS required taxpayers with foreign financial accounts exceeding $10,000 to file electronically through the Bank Secrecy Act E-File System.

In addition to recognizing the tax administration challenges presented by cross-border transactions, the IRS continued to focus on providing service to return preparers. Return preparers play a key role in increasing taxpayer compliance and strengthening the integrity of the U.S. tax system.

The IRS required anyone who prepared or assisted in preparing federal tax returns for compensation to have a valid Preparer Tax Identification Number (PTIN). In FY 2013, the IRS held a successful PTIN renewal season offering enhanced PTIN system usability, troubleshooting tips, and other tools, resulting in over 76,000 fewer telephone inquiries answered during the peak season. As of September 30, 2013, there were 689,865 valid PTINs.

In FY 2013, the IRS continued to educate and inform paid return preparers on tax law compliance by:

- Conducting educational visitations with return preparers to assist them in completing and filing tax returns.

- Visiting over 3,000 return preparers nationally, including 300 real-time EITC compliance visits, to focus on due diligence requirements for EITC and Form 1040 preparation, Circular 230 responsibilities, PTIN requirements, Schedule C preparation, and the consequences of preparing inaccurate returns.

- Addressing egregious preparers through a variety of methods to ensure appropriate penalties and/or sanctions were pursued. Sixty-two injunctions (permanent or preliminary) were obtained.

In support of the Return Preparer Program (RPP), the IRS committed resources to maximize the impact of criminal enforcement through education, outreach, and a coordinated cross-functional publicity strategy. The RPP performance accomplishments in FY 2013 included:

- 309 RPP criminal investigation initiations.
- 372 RPP criminal investigation completions.
- 207 RPP convictions.
- 97.2% conviction rate on RPP criminal investigations.
- 93.0% publicity rate on RPP adjudicated cases.
- 110 EITC Knock and Talk Visits with identified at-risk return preparers.
- 23 RPP-related outreach events held for tax and accounting practitioners, the general public, and the media.

The IRS takes appropriate enforcement action against taxpayers who file fraudulently. The IRS criminal investigation program examines potential criminal violations of the Internal Revenue Code and related financial crimes such as money laundering, currency violations, tax-related identity theft fraud, and terrorist financing that adversely affect tax administration. In FY 2013, the IRS:

13

INTERNAL REVENUE SERVICE
Management's Discussion & Analysis
Fiscal Year 2013

- Completed 5,557 criminal investigations.
- Achieved a conviction rate of 93.1%.
- Maintained a Department of Justice acceptance rate of 95.5%, with a U.S. Attorney acceptance rate of 93.4%, which compares favorably with other federal law enforcement agencies.
- Obtained 3,311 convictions.

The IRS continued identifying and stopping fraudulent return filings and refunds. The Questionable Refund Program (QRP) and the Income Verification Operations (IVO) program, (formerly Accounts Management Taxpayer Assurance Program (AMTAP)) identify questionable refunds where individuals file fictitious tax returns claiming refunds based on false information such as federal income tax withholdings or refundable credits. In FY 2013, the IRS:

- Stopped 2.48 million fraudulent returns with associated refunds of $15.2 billion under the Integrity and Verification Operations (IVO) program.
- Identified 1,992 QRP schemes comprised of 1,638,357 individual tax returns with more than $9.5 billion in potentially fraudulent refunds.
- Initiated 1,513 investigations, achieved a 96.0% conviction rate, and an 89.3% publicity rate on adjudicated cases.

The IRS released the final report on the colleges and universities study, which resulted in more than 180 revisions made to unrelated business income (UBI) that was reported for more than 30 different colleges and universities activities. Examination highlights include:

- Increases to unrelated business taxable income (UBTI) for 90% of colleges and universities examined, totaling approximately $90 million.
- Disallowance of more than $170 million in losses and net operating losses, which could amount to more than $60 million in assessed taxes.
- Increases in wages of more than $1 million and the assessment of more than $200,000 in taxes and penalties relating to retirement plan issues of employees at the colleges and universities examined.

**Strategic Goal 2 Performance Measures**

While IRS was not able to achieve all of its targets, the accuracy or quality of our results were mostly not impacted by the drastic reductions to funding.

The IRS met 71% (12 of 17) enforcement performance measures in FY 2013.

**Strategic Goal 2: Enforce the Law to Ensure Everyone Meets Their Obligation to Pay Taxes**

| | FY 2013 | |
| --- | --- | --- |
| | Target | Actual |
| Examination Coverage – Individual | 1.0% | 1.0% |
| Field Examination National Quality Review Score | 86.9% | 89.2% |
| Office Examination National Quality Review Score | 91.1% | 90.3% |
| Examination Quality – Large Business[1] | Baseline | 92.0% |
| Examination Coverage – Business (assets >$10M) | 4.6% | 5.6% |
| Examination Efficiency – Individual (1040) | 145 | 142 |

14

INTERNAL REVENUE SERVICE
Management's Discussion & Analysis
Fiscal Year 2013

| | | |
|---|---|---|
| Automated Underreporter (AUR) Efficiency | 2,035 | 2,025 |
| Automated Underreporter (AUR) Coverage | 2.9% | 2.8% |
| Collection Coverage – Units | 46.4% | 47.0% |
| Collection Efficiency – Units | 2,049 | 2,057 |
| Field Collection National Quality Review Score | 80.4% | 81.4% |
| Automated Collection System (ACS) Accuracy | 94.5% | 94.4% |
| Criminal Investigations Completed | 4,350 | 5,557 |
| Number of Convictions | 2,400 | 3,311 |
| Conviction Rate | 92.0% | 93.1% |
| Conviction Efficiency Rate ($) | $285,000 | $211,048 |
| TE/GE Determination Case Closures | 62,473 | 65,877 |

¹ As a result of program changes that occurred in the Large Business and International (LB&I) organization, starting in FY 2013, a new Examination Quality - Large Business measure will replace the two previous LB&I quality measures - Examination Quality - Industry and Coordinated Industry

**Shortfall Explanations -** The impact of late legislation enacted in January 2013 and the effects of sequestration were significant impediments to the ability of the IRS to achieve all enforcement goals. IRS funding for enforcement was decreased over $350 million in FY 2013 from FY 2012 as a result of sequestration.

**Office Examination National Quality Review Score**: Office exam showed an increase in 9 of the 17 quality attributes. Exam continues to work to improve the weakest quality attributes. Efforts to improve quality included: distributing education packets to examiners and managers that provided scenarios and solutions for some of exam's quality challenges; and, issuing interim guidance memos focusing on National Time Frames, Pre-Contact Responsibilities, and the setting of Mutual Commitment Dates.

**Exam Efficiency – Individual (1040)**: While closing over 1.4 million individual audits for the 5th consecutive year, Exam efficiency increased was not met due to budgetary challenges, more complex paid preparer cases, and delays in closing cases due to Hurricane Sandy.

**Automated Underreporter (AUR) Efficiency**: While closing over 4.1 million cases for the 4th consecutive year, AUR efficiency was not met due to budgetary challenges and shifting of resources to address non-closure type work such as identity theft.

**Automated Underreporter (AUR) Coverage**: Total contact closures decreased 9.0% while individual filings increased by 1.8% in the FY 2013 compared to last year. However, because of budgetary challenges faced during the year and resources being diverted to Identity Theft, the target was missed by roughly 3.0%

**Automated Collection System (ACS) Accuracy**: All sites continued efforts to address the issues impacting Customer Accuracy, including identifying the top drivers impacting Customer Accuracy and sharing and discussing these trends with all levels of management for proper changes. In addition, mandatory use of several of the Interactive Tax Assistant Tools became effective June 17th which helped reduce Customer Accuracy errors.

**STRATEGIC FOUNDATIONS: Invest for high performance**

The IRS must invest in its strategic foundations to achieve its goals. IRS employees are the most valuable asset in effective tax administration. Without a high-quality and dedicated workforce, the IRS cannot tackle the risks posed by an increasingly complex external

15

INTERNAL REVENUE SERVICE
Management's Discussion & Analysis
Fiscal Year 2013

environment. To ensure that IRS meets the challenges of tax administration, we must provide our employees with world-class technology systems, processes, and tools.

**Strategic Foundation Facts**

- Delivered more than 200 filing season applications and modernization projects.
- Received more than 240 million Fed/State returns from 35 participating states through Modernized e-File (MeF).
- Refreshed over 5,470 employee laptops and 1,087 desktops.
- Produced over 370 advisories and bulletins informing users of mitigation actions to address vulnerabilities and threats that impacted IRS systems.
- Completed 11,034 Freedom of Information Act cases, closing cases within an average of 17 days.
- Achieved a Telework participation rate of 26%, exceeding the 24% goal.
- Exceeded the New Hire for people with disability goal of 10% by achieving 13.29%.
- Exceeded the New Hire for people with targeted disabilities goal of 2% by achieving 2.23%.
- Increased external hiring by 14%, 7,385 compared to 6,471 in FY 2012.
- Received 463,532 applications, and processed almost 80,000 competitive and non-competitive personnel actions.

The IRS values its workforce and recognizes human capital as its most important resource. This is critical in the efforts to make significant progress toward achieving the strategic objective of making the IRS the best place to work in government, ensuring meaningful improvements to employee engagement, and developing a quality workforce to meet future challenges.

The results of the OPM Federal Employee Viewpoint survey showed that the IRS ranked highly in the following engagement indicators when compared to 15 large agencies:

- Second in Leadership & Knowledge Management.
- Third in Employee Engagement.
- Third in Results-Oriented Performance Culture.
- Fourth in Talent Management.

In FY 2013, the IRS continued to identify opportunities to use low-cost recognition and reward tools to recognize employee achievements and boost employee engagement, which included:

- Issuing 8,601 ShoutOut! forum messages, which recognize or thank an employee for their recent contributions or actions.
- Sending 76,705 eCards, an increase of 58 percent over FY 2012.
- Creating and publishing over 300 new styles of eCards.
- Encouraging increased recognition during Public Service Recognition Week, when employees sent 3,748 e-Cards and 1,400 ShoutOuts! and during Administrative Professionals Week, when employees sent 5,817 e-Cards and 787 ShoutOuts!

The IRS increased Geographic Leadership Communities (GLCs) throughout the nation. Thirty-two cross-functional GLCs sponsored by executives, senior managers, and frontline managers have been launched to identify and support emerging leaders, host developmental opportunities

16

INTERNAL REVENUE SERVICE
Management's Discussion & Analysis
Fiscal Year 2013

and skill-building workshops, and increase employee engagement while leveraging talent and resources.

Focusing on its workforce and leadership, the IRS continued to make strides in employee development:

- Marketed Learn and Lead 24x7, a searchable online library of topics for skills development that includes courses accredited by the American Council on Education (ACE), reducing in-person training travel costs. 327,614 courses were completed in FY 2013, an increase of 21.3% from FY 2012.

- Completed the Treasury Competency Assessment Process (TCAP) for over 1,150 human resources professionals and virtual training for over 5,000 employees in the Administrative Career Enhancement Program.

- Launched the College Credit Program in partnership with Skillsoft and the American Council on Education (ACE) to provide IRS employees the opportunity to earn academic college credit in 40 online college-level course topics from over 500 course titles. Employees who pass an IRS-proctored exam are eligible to receive college credit. In FY 2013, 11 IRS sites were approved to administer final exams in accordance with ACE requirements. Employees completed over 1,000 ACE college credit courses.

- Continued the Leadership Succession Review (LSR) program to ensure a strong, cohesive leadership development and succession planning approach from frontline to executive development. Managers and employees who seek to become managers assess their leadership competencies, identify professional goals, and develop their talents to achieve those goals. Almost 22,000 employees with an interest in management positions participated. The IRS broadcasted seven Leadership Skill Building Webinars, which focused on areas of need identified through the LSR process.

The IRS leveraged employee knowledge, skills, and experience across the organization through a comprehensive management strategy focused on knowledge sharing between employees:

- Continued the Issue Practice Group (IPG) project. IPGs are comprised of subject matter experts that develop and maintain technical expertise and share knowledge to ensure consistency in how the IRS addresses industry issues. There were 9,164 inquiries since the project's inception, and as of September 30, 2013, there were 395 inquiries in process, eight inquiries assigned, and five inquiries awaiting assignment.

- Established 18 International Practice Networks (IPNs) to facilitate knowledge sharing among employees and to direct the IRS International strategy, training, and data management.

The IRS enhanced its hiring processes by:

- Decreasing the overall hiring cycle time to 67 days, which is below the Office of the Personnel Management and Department of the Treasury requirement of 80 days. The decrease in hiring cycle time resulted in the timely hiring of 6,909 critical positions during Filing Season.

17

INTERNAL REVENUE SERVICE
Management's Discussion & Analysis
Fiscal Year 2013

- Achieving a 7.07% hiring rate of disabled veterans, surpassing the 4.92% goal.

- Transitioning 187 students to the Pathways Program, a new program that replaced and enhanced all former student hiring programs.

In addition to investing in employees, the IRS also invested heavily in information technology (IT) services and solutions. IRS modernization efforts continued to focus on building and deploying advanced IT systems, processes, and tools to improve efficiency and productivity. FY 2013 modernization successes included:

- Customer Account Data Engine 2 (CADE 2). In Filing Season 2013, CADE 2 posted over 139 million returns and issued over 111 million refunds totaling $281 billion. Daily processing and posting of individual taxpayer accounts enabled faster refunds (65.47% compared to 30% in 2011 (pre-CADE 2)).

- Modernized e-File (MeF). MeF Release 8 deployed for Filing Season 2013, which implemented performance-tuning, stabilization, and monitoring to ensure that support of the increased volume of e-file returns. For the first time ever, MeF was the sole e-file platform used for the Filing Season, as the IRS processed 224.7 million individual federal and state returns, and 16.8 million Business Master File returns.

- Electronic Fraud Detection System (EFDS). The IRS deployed a new MeF/EFDS interface in FY 2013, ensuring EFDS completed fraud detection before further processing. In FY 2013, EFDS processed over 138 million returns and stopped over $10 billion in fraudulent refunds.

- Information Return Document Matching (IRDM). In January 2013, IRDM's full Case Management functionality became available for casework. Case management matches new information returns (e.g., 1099-K) with both individual and business tax returns to identify potential income under reporting.

- IRS.gov Portal. The IRS transitioned one of the two internet portals used to access IRS.gov, the Public User Portal (PUP), to the new Integrated Enterprise Portal (IEP) environment allowing the IRS to increase IT services to meet taxpayers' changing needs. In FY 2013, the new IEP has accommodated a 22% increase in visits and a 6% increase in page views compared to FY 2012.

Since Fiscal Year 2010, the IRS has made a concerted effort to identify and put in place ways of saving taxpayer dollars and working more efficiently. As a result, IRS actions taken in the last two years have had savings of more than $350 million. Some examples of the ways that the IRS achieved cost savings included:

- Released 557,000 square feet for an annual total rent savings of $15.7 million.

- Renewed 43,275 employee SmartID cards in FY 2013, resulting in a cost avoidance of approximately $1.3 million. Additionally, the IRS rekeyed more than 10,800 employee and contractor SmartID cards resulting in a cost avoidance of $325,000.

18

INTERNAL REVENUE SERVICE
Management's Discussion & Analysis
Fiscal Year 2013

- Continued program efficiencies through Lean Six Sigma (LSS) processes. The IRS applied the LSS methodology to processes in the Worker's Compensation Branch resulted in 27 process improvements and a first year efficiency savings of $81,000.

- Reduced the service-wide training budget by 76% compared to FY 2012. With over 94% of training delivered online, employees were guaranteed opportunities to enhance skills and development, while focusing on cost savings.

- Deployed Enterprise E-Fax (EEFax) giving employees the ability to send and receive electronic fax documents directly from their workstations. EEFax increases productivity, enhances information exchanges, and helps the IRS "Go Green" by transmitting documents in digital format, rather than paper.

The IRS collects a tremendous amount of sensitive information, and protecting this information is vital to maintaining the public trust. In FY 2013, the IRS monitored, identified, and mitigated fraudulent schemes, to protect hardware, software, and taxpayers' information from increasing and evolving online fraud and identity theft schemes. The IRS improved threat intelligence gathering capabilities to quickly take down servers and web sites that were sending out fraudulent emails aimed at defrauding innocent taxpayers. In FY 2013, the IRS:

- Identified, mitigated, and responded to more than 1,300 cyber incidents and blocked over 5,800 websites to prevent access to malicious or compromised sites.

- Eliminated 3,119 fraudulent domestic websites including 2,790 fraudulent malware websites.

- Reduced the average elapsed time to notify taxpayers of a data loss from 48.4 days in FY 2012 to 40.8 days in FY 2013, a 15.7% decrease.

- Implemented a Safeguarding Personally Identifiable Information Data Extracts (SPIIDE) project to advance data protection and reduce inadvertent disclosures.

- Established a means for the IRS to systematically identify and categorize all personally identifiable information (PII) to ensure it is properly labeled and protected by implementing the PII Inventory and Classification Project (PIIC).

- Recognized and quickly shut down 3,542 phishing websites.

The IRS continued efforts to increase collaboration with states on identity theft, fraudulent refunds, and the transmission of leads from the states to the IRS. FY 2013 efforts included:

- Taxpayer Identification Number (TIN) Matching Program. The IRS developed an initiative enabling states to use information from the TIN Matching program to validate TINs on returns with refund claims to prevent refund fraud. Twenty-three states and the District of Columbia have signed on participate in this program.

- State Audit Report Program (SARP). The IRS processed 33,186 cases and assessed $671 million based upon information exchanged through SARP that uses monthly state audit report data to support compliance processes.

19

INTERNAL REVENUE SERVICE
Management's Discussion & Analysis
Fiscal Year 2013

- State Income Tax Levy Program (SITLP). SITLP continues to successfully collect unpaid taxes through 35 participating states. This automated levy program collected over $192 million to date, an increase from $168.4 million in FY 2012.

**Strategic Foundations Performance Measures**

The IRS did not meet its Business System Modernization targets in FY 2013. The target is set at 90% of projects achieving the final schedule and costing that was within 10% of the original project. Due to the number of projects being below 10, if one project misses a schedule or cost by 10% that means the entire measure missed the target.

**Strategic Foundations: Invest for High Performance**

| Performance Measure | FY 2013 Target | FY 2013 Actual |
|---|---|---|
| Percent of BSM Projects within +/- 10% Cost Variance | 90.0% | 0% |
| Percent of BSM Projects within +/- 10% Schedule Variance | 90.0% | 83.3% |

**Shortfall Explanations**

**Percent of BSM Projects within +/- 10% Cost Variance E:** Zero out of six BSM project segments met the cost variance threshold. Three of the segments actually came in lower than the projected costs. Additional funds were needed to support database implementation activities and to support unplanned and unfunded software/hardware costs along with costs for updating and maintaining system forms in order to be in compliance with IRS standards. These costs were not expected when the target was set, causing the cost variance to fall outside of the original 10% variance of the planned cost projects.

**Percent of BSM Projects within +/- 10% Schedule Variance E:** Five out of six BSM project segments (83.3%) planned for deliveries during FY 2013 met the schedule variance threshold. CADE 2 TS1 milestone 5 exit was delayed due to an unforeseen slow-down because of huge volumes generated by taxpayer identification number updates to the database.

**PROGRESS MADE ON TAX-RELATED IDENTITY THEFT**

Identity theft continues to grow and touches nearly every part of the IRS. In FY 2013, the IRS continued to focus on a comprehensive and aggressive strategy to identify and combat tax-related identity theft. The strategy included 1) preventing refund fraud caused by identity theft, 2) investigating and initiating criminal recourse against perpetrators of refund fraud caused by identity theft, and 3) assisting taxpayers victimized by identity theft. FY 2013 efforts included:

1) Preventing federal income tax refund fraud caused by identity theft.

- Deployed the Identity Protection Personal Identification Number (IP PIN) to over 770,000 taxpayers for the 2013 filing season. The IP PIN is a unique identifier that shows that a particular taxpayer is the rightful filer of the return and allows these individuals to avoid delays in filing returns and receiving refunds.

20

- Increased the number of employees dedicated to preventing refund fraud and assisting taxpayers victimized by identity theft to 3,000, more than twice the number of employees in FY 2012.

- Masked social security numbers (SSNs) using a two-dimensional (2D) barcode on 12 additional nonpayment notices, for a total of 58 nonpayment notices and 106 payment notices, affecting 20.4 million and 97.3 million annual taxpayer notices, respectively.

- Partnered with the United States Postal Inspection Service (USPIS) and other law enforcement partners to recover over 24,000 U.S. Treasury tax refund checks issued in connection with returns associated with identity theft, thereby securing over $105 million in funds.

- Conducted 191 Identity Theft outreach events with tax and accounting practitioners, the general public, and the media.

- Hosted an Identity Theft Summit with law enforcement members from 14 federal agencies to discuss ways to strengthen collaborative efforts amongst agencies in the fight against identity theft. .

- Expanded data exchange agreements with federal and state law enforcement officials to implement aggressive actions to address identity theft. The IRS began transmission of the data to two participating states in 2013 resulting in the sharing of over 575,000 records of identity theft victims in California and New York.

- Prevented fraudulent refunds through the Prisoner Initiative, which focused on detection, selection, resolution, and prevention of prisoner fraudulent filing activity:

    o Stopped ID theft by prisoners who filed false returns using fraudulent or stolen information through the Blue Bag Program, where the IRS and prisons cooperate to monitor inmates' tax-related communications to deter inmate tax fraud. Historically, prisons mailed inmates' tax-related documents to the IRS in IRS-supplied blue bags, giving rise to the Blue Bag Program. Today, those bags have given way to other secure mailing media, but the program name remains. In FY 2013, the IRS stopped 163,780 returns totaling over $1.17 billion. The IRS protected over $18 billion in revenue and referred over $10.8 billion in false claims to the frivolous filer unit. There are 995 institutions participating in the Blue Bag Program.

    o Implemented legislation for state and federal correctional agencies to annually provide the IRS with inmate data.

    o Improved the 2013 Prisoner File compilation process by improving the accuracy of the file by addressing structural formatting and variance errors. Mismatched and deceased taxpayer files were made available for the first time this year.

21

o   Expanded the number and quality of identity screening filters, and suspended or rejected more than 4.6 million suspicious returns so far this year, which approaches the 5 million for all of last year.

2) Investigating and initiating criminal recourse against perpetrators of refund fraud caused by identity theft.

- Launched the Law Enforcement Assistance Program (LEAP) nationwide, which increased efforts to combat refund fraud by working with state and local law enforcement agencies to provide taxpayer consent to access their tax return data vital to investigating and prosecuting identity thieves. The program allowed victimized taxpayers to sign a waiver (Form 8821-A) authorizing the release of any tax information to the designated state or local law enforcement official pursuing the investigation. In FY 2013, 314 state/local law enforcement agencies from 35 states participated in the program, resulting in 2,481 waiver requests for taxpayer consent to access their tax return data. Since the program's inception in FY 2012, the IRS received 3,686 requests.

- Collaborated with the Department of Justice's Tax Division and local U.S. Attorneys' offices throughout the United States to conduct coordinated identity theft sweeps nationwide. These sweeps resulted in 734 enforcement actions related to identity theft and refund fraud and involved 389 individuals, 109 arrests, 48 search warrants, and 189 indictments and criminal complaints.

- Launched more than 1,492 identity theft criminal investigations, a 66% increase from FY 2012.

- Continued to develop and refer identity theft refund fraud schemes for investigation through the Identity Theft Clearinghouse (ITC). In FY 2013, the ITC received 1,426 identity theft refund fraud leads, involving over 391,000 tax returns with over $1.3 billion in requested refunds.

- Collaborated with the Department of Justice Tax Division to issue a new directive, which provides the United States Attorney the authority to expeditiously and efficiently work stolen identity refund fraud investigations.

3) Assisting taxpayers victimized by identity theft.

- Trained 35,000 employees to work with taxpayers and help them tackle their identity theft incidents.

- Worked with victims to resolve and close more than 565,000 identity theft cases, more than three times the number of cases resolved last year.

- Centralized victims' lists and information forwarded to IRS by other Federal, State, and local agencies during nationwide investigative efforts using a Data Processing Center (DPC) Identity Theft Victims List Process. The information allowed IRS employees to analyze and make necessary adjustments to accounts of taxpayers

22

that are likely targets of identity theft. In FY 2013, the DPC processed over 70% more identity theft records compared to FY 2012.

- Resolved refund issues for taxpayers who became victims this year in less than an average of 53 days, faster than in previous years.

## IMPLEMENTING TAX-RELATED PROVISIONS OF THE AFFORDABLE CARE ACT

The Affordable Care Act (ACA) represented the largest and most complex set of tax law changes in more than 20 years, with more than 40 provisions amending the tax laws. While many of the provisions go into effect over several years, the IRS had to take immediate action on several of the provisions that are already in effect. The IRS:

- Collected more than $2.6 billion for the Branded Prescription Drug fee.

- Provided more than $1.4 billion to businesses through the small business tax credit since the credit was implemented in FY 2010.

- Published *Healthcare Law Online Resources* (Pub. 5093), which provided internet resources from federal agency partners including the Department of Health and Human Services (HHS), the Department of Labor and the Small Business Administration.

- Created a new ACA web page, which explained the tax benefits and responsibilities for individuals, families, and employers, as well as provides information regarding taxpayers' health insurance choices and how they may affect tax returns filed in 2015.

- Launched two new IT services for Marketplace exchanges, providing both income and family size data and an optional computation service for exchanges to determine the maximum Advance Premium Tax Credit

- Developed an ACA speaker's cadre that included speakers throughout the IRS who manage stakeholder outreach and education requests related to ACA tax law implementation during the 2013 Health Insurance Marketplace pre-enrollment and enrollment period.

- Conducted separate ACA sessions at an IRS Nationwide Tax Forum providing information on health care-related tax provisions for individuals and businesses, details about provisions that may affect taxpayers in 2013, and a preview of provisions beginning in 2014.

- Published regulations and other guidance on requirements for tax-exempt hospitals, the Patient-Centered Outcomes Research Institute fee, the health insurance providers' fee, and the small business health care tax credit.

- Completed the first cycle of hospital reviews by evaluating the community benefit activities of charitable hospitals, closing 1,141 reviews.

- Approved 19 applications received for recognition of tax-exempt status from Qualified

23

Nonprofit Health Insurance Issuers (501(c) (29), CO-OP program participants).

- Closed 625 exempt organization examinations to determine eligibility for small business health care credits, resulting in $1,387,571 assessed overall or $2,206 per return.

- Met with HHS and discussed the impact of ACA provisions on Indian Tribal Governments, tribal employers, and tribal members. Conducted 20 ACA outreach events focused on governmental entities, tax-exempt organizations, and Indian tribes.

## SYSTEMS CONTROLS AND LEGAL COMPLIANCE

The IRS continued to enhance financial management and appropriate controls that are an integral component of all IRS programs.

### Federal Managers' Financial Integrity Act (FMFIA)

The IRS provides qualified assurance that the systems of management control objectives, in accordance with the internal control requirements of the Federal Managers' Financial Integrity Act (FMFIA), the Federal Financial Management Improvement Act (FFMIA), the Office of Management and Budget (OMB) Circular A-123, the Government Charge Card Abuse Prevention Act of 2012, and the Reports Consolidation Act of 2000, were achieved during FY 2013. Organizations are operating in accordance with the procedures and standards prescribed by the Comptroller General and OMB guidelines.

The systems of management control for the IRS organizations are designed to ensure that:

- Programs achieve their intended results.
- Resources are used consistent with the overall mission.
- Programs and resources are free from waste, fraud, and mismanagement.
- Laws and regulations are followed.
- Controls are sufficient to minimize improper and erroneous payments.
- Performance information is reliable.
- System security is in substantial compliance with all relevant requirements.
- Continuity of operations planning in critical areas is sufficient to reduce risk to reasonable levels.
- Financial management systems are in compliance with federal financial systems standards, i.e., FMFIA Section 4 and FFMIA.

The qualified assurance is based on the fact that the IRS has a material weakness in internal control over financial reporting and the financial management systems do not substantially comply with FFMIA. This assurance is provided relative to FMFIA Sections 2 and 4.

The IRS is monitoring the following material weakness in internal control over financial reporting and the corresponding corrective action plan:

- Unpaid Tax Assessments

24

INTERNAL REVENUE SERVICE
Management's Discussion & Analysis
Fiscal Year 2013

## Federal Financial Management Improvement Act (FFMIA)

To address the Unpaid Tax Assessments material weakness, the IRS implemented programming changes in the Custodial Detail Data Base to improve the financial classification in situations where:

- A portion of the assessment on a business related return has expired by statute.
- A taxpayer is ordered to make restitution on criminal activity.
- A taxpayer has become a victim of identity theft and his/her account has been compromised. The taxpayer's account will be restored to its accurate balance.

In addition, the IRS continues to update the Automated Trust Fund Recovery system to increase the number of Trust Fund Recovery Penalty (TFRP) cases that can be worked without user intervention and to eliminate errors. The IRS will continue to perform internal control testing to ensure the accuracy of these accounts.

## Government Charge Card Abuse Prevention Act of 2012

In accordance with the requirements of the Government Charge Card Abuse Prevention Act of 2012, the IRS provides assurance that its internal control over the use of government charge cards was effective. Specifically, the IRS complied with the Department of Treasury Charge Card Management Plan and provided agency-wide purchase card guidance for the proper use of government charge cards. IRS monitors charge card activity to validate that the appropriate policies and procedures are being followed and ensures that corrective actions have been taken to mitigate the risk of fraud and inappropriate charge card practices.

## Reports Consolidation Act of 2000

In accordance with the Reports Consolidation Act of 2000, the IRS provides assurance that the IRS Critical Performance Measures are reliable. Internal Revenue Manual 1.5.1, "Managing Statistics in a Balanced Measurement System, The IRS Balanced Performance Measurement System," provides a detailed template that documents each measure's definition, formula, reliability, and reporting frequency. These controls verify that performance data is consistently and accurately collected over time.

## Continuity of Operations (COOP)

The IRS enhanced its disaster recovery program by incorporating critical business processes and system infrastructure into Information System Contingency Plans and ensuring that each plan has a documented Business Impact Analysis. The IRS validated that each Information System Contingency Plan for all FISMA master inventory systems contained keystroke recovery procedures for each asset and ensured that each plan was updated and tested annually. The IRS conducted over 300 exercises and tests to determine that the plans were current and executable, back up data was readily available and readable, and Critical Infrastructure Protection systems could be recovered within their defined Recovery Time Objective. To mitigate the highest risk and promote cost effectiveness, the IRS prioritized the systems' infrastructure single points of failure to identify the most beneficial remediation investments that reinforced the downgrade of the disaster recovery area of the Information Security material weakness.

25

## Limitations of Financial Statements

The principal financial statements have been prepared to report the results of IRS operations, pursuant to the requirements of 31 U.S.C. 3515(b). The statements were prepared from the books and records of the IRS in accordance with generally accepted accounting principles for Federal entities and the format prescribed by OMB. The statements are in addition to the financial reports used to monitor and control budgetary resources, which are prepared from the same books and records. The statements should be read with the realization that the IRS is a component of the U.S. Government, a sovereign entity.

## OMB Circular A-123, "Management's Responsibility for Internal Control"

IRS management is responsible for establishing and maintaining adequate internal control over financial reporting, which includes safeguarding of assets and compliance with applicable laws and regulations. The IRS conducted the required evaluation of the effectiveness of its internal control over financial reporting in accordance with OMB Circular A-123, Management's Responsibility for Internal Control. Based on the results of this evaluation, the IRS provides qualified assurance that its internal control over financial reporting was operating effectively as of September 30, 2013.

The FY 2013 OMB Circular A-123 testing included the following activities:

- Tested internal control sets for the 23 transaction processes identified by the Department of the Treasury that are material to its Consolidated Financial Statements. The tests included 14 administrative processes covering material portions of the $12 billion in annual administrative transactions, 6 information system processes, and 3 custodial processes covering material portions of the over $2.9 trillion in tax revenue receipts through September 30, 2013. The transactions included additional testing for custodial activity related to tax refunds and cash reconciliation. The testing indicated the internal controls were primarily in place and operating effectively with no new material weaknesses found in the design or operation of the internal controls.

- Tested the compensating procedures used to produce the annually audited financial statements.

- Performed supplemental testing of the FY 2013 transactions during the fourth quarter to verify that controls remained effective throughout the year.

- Reviewed controls over financial reporting and determined that controls are in place and effective.

- Conducted a self-assessment of the IRS internal control environment using an Abbreviated Internal Control Evaluation Checklist authored by GAO.

- Reviewed IRS compliance with applicable laws and regulatory requirements regarding financial reporting and internal control, including compliance with FFMIA, FMFIA, FISMA, the Improper Payments Elimination and Recovery Act, and the Chief Financial Officers Act, determining that the IRS is in compliance except for the issues identified in this assurance statement.

26

## Federal Information Security Management Act (FISMA)

In accordance with the requirements of the Federal Information Security Management Act (FISMA), the IRS maintained an agency-wide information security program and provided a comprehensive framework for validating the effectiveness of information security controls over resources that support IRS business operations and goals. Specifically, the IRS inventory of FISMA reportable systems is compliant with security requirements from OMB, the National Institute of Standards and Technology, the Department of the Treasury, and IRS internal policies. These systems have completed annual security control testing, participated in required security authorization and assessment activities, and have timely addressed all

| Actions | Status |
|---|---|
| Security Assessment and Authorization of Systems | 100% |
| Systems Accreditation | 100% |
| Specialized Training | 99% |
| Annual Awareness Training | 99% |
| Contractor Systems Reviews | 100% |
| Annual Security Controls Testing | 100% |
| Information Systems Contingency Plan Testing | 100% |
| Privacy Impact Assessment | 100% |
| System of Record Notice | 100% |

required Plans of Actions and Milestones (POA&M) for identified weaknesses. Additionally, IRS met or exceeded all FISMA goals for 2013 including the timely closure of 98% of all POA&M items due, 99% compliance for specialized employee IT security training requirements, and 100% Information Systems Contingency Plan testing for all reportable FISMA assets for the sixth consecutive year.

## Downgrade of the Information Security Material Weakness

In the IRS Fiscal Years 2012 and 2011 Financial Statements audit report, the Government Accountability Office (GAO) noted, "IRS continued to make important progress in addressing its deficiencies in internal control. Specifically, based on IRS's success in addressing numerous deficiencies in its information security controls over its financial reporting systems, GAO considers information security, previously reported as a long-standing material weakness, to be a significant deficiency that warrants the attention of those charged with governance of IRS."

Recognizing the larger scope of IRS's work as a result of FMFIA requirements and management's responsibilities for the integrity of IRS controls, IRS continued to carry Information Security as an internal material weakness with the goal of downgrade in FY 2013. To support the IRS downgrade of this internally-carried material weakness, IRS performed a self-assessment of its internal controls for systems that impact the financial statements and demonstrated that management, technical, and operational controls are in place and effective to secure the IRS infrastructure.

On June 28, 2013, the Financial and Management Controls Executive Steering Committee (FMC ESC), who oversees the material weakness remediation plan, voted unanimously to downgrade the internally-carried Information Security material weakness to a significant deficiency. GAO and the Treasury Inspector General for Tax Administration (TIGTA) have been informed of IRS actions to downgrade the material weakness to a significant deficiency.

The key accomplishments in addressing this material weakness were:

27

- Complied with the Federal Information Security Management Act (FISMA), the Office of Management and Budget (OMB), the National Institute of Standards and Technology (NIST), the Department of the Treasury, and IRS security requirements.

- Established a cross-functional working group to test and validate corrective actions to address the weakness and prevent premature closure.

- Provided evidence and assurance of continuous monitoring and controls for Information Technology (IT) systems owned or operated by external entities for risks to IRS financial systems or access to taxpayer or other sensitive information the IRS maintains.

- Developed continuous monitoring activities and updated internal policies and procedures.

- Identified material administrative and custodial revenue transactions significant to the IRS-wide financial statements.

- Evaluated internal control effectiveness over financial reporting in accordance with OMB Circular A-123 for transaction processes material to Department of the Treasury's Consolidated Financial Statements.

## Progress Made on Significant Deficiencies

In FY 2013, IRS closed the Collection of Unpaid Taxes and Tax Refund Disbursements Significant Deficiencies.

## Major Management Challenges and High-Risk Areas

GAO and TIGTA identified several Management Challenges and High-Risk Areas facing the IRS. The following is the management and performance challenge identified by GAO in its 2013 High Risk Series Update and by TIGTA in its October 15, 2012, memorandum titled Management and Performance Challenges Facing the Internal Revenue Service for Fiscal Year 2013.

### GAO High Risk Areas for IRS

- Enforcement of Tax Laws

Sufficient progress was made to remove Business Systems Modernization as a high-risk designation.

After 18 years, in February 2013, the Government Accountability Office (GAO) removed the IRS Business Systems Modernization program from its High-Risk List. GAO concluded that the IRS made substantial progress in addressing security material weaknesses over the past several years and demonstrated a commitment to sustained progress. The IRS has in place about 80 percent of the practices needed for an effective investment management process, including all of the processes needed for effective project oversight. In addition, the IRS improved its software development practices using the Carnegie Mellon University Software Engineering Institute's Capability Maturity Model Integration (CMMI), which calls for standard and disciplined

28

INTERNAL REVENUE SERVICE
Management's Discussion & Analysis
Fiscal Year 2013

software development and acquisition practices to dramatically improve quality and increase capacity. In September 2012, the IRS Information Technology (IT) organization reached CMMI maturity level 3, which the GAO acknowledges as a high achievement by industry standards. In December of 2013, the IT organization achieved Information Technology Infrastructure Library (ITIL) certification level 3. ITIL is a set of standard IT operations practices, processes and procedures. It reflects IT industry best practices.

**TIGTA Management Challenges**

1. Security for Taxpayer Data and Employees
2. Tax Compliance Initiatives
3. Modernization
4. Implementing the Affordable Care Act and Other Tax Law Changes
5. Fraudulent Claims and Improper Payments
6. Providing Quality Taxpayer Service Operations
7. Human Capital
8. Globalization
9. Taxpayer Protection and Rights
10. Achieving Program Efficiencies and Cost Savings

The IRS is addressing these issues through its existing program activities. Measures of these program activities serve to show progress in addressing the management challenges and high-risk areas. Summarized below are the major management and performance challenges facing the IRS and information on the actions taken in fiscal year 2013 and planned for fiscal year 2014 and beyond.

**1. SECURITY FOR TAXPAYER DATA AND EMPLOYEES**

**Summary of Major Issues:** Promote measures for appropriate physical security and protection of financial, personal, and other information.

**Actions Taken:**

- Masked social security numbers (SSNs) using a two-dimensional (2D) barcode on 12 additional nonpayment notices, for a total of 58 nonpayment notices and 106 payment notices, affecting 20.4 million and 97.3 million annual taxpayer notices, respectively.
- Issued Identity Protection Personal Identification Numbers (IP PINs) to more than 770,000 taxpayers for the 2013 filing season. The IP PIN is a unique identifier that shows that a particular taxpayer is the rightful filer of the return and allows these individuals to avoid delays in filing returns and receiving refunds.
- Developed additional levels of security to the existing e-Auth system for IRS online applications, such as third-party identification data, which required taxpayers to prove who they are before accessing the IRS application. Nearly 175,000 callers leveraged the third party ID proofing process for the following IRS online applications:
    - Guest Access for tax filers not wishing to register with the IRS.
    - Two-factor authentication to strengthen security for online taxpayers beyond the ID and password.
    - Infrastructure improvements to enhance performance, usability, and security.
    - Reporting to include application specific reports, taxpayer account reports, and system infrastructure reports.

29

INTERNAL REVENUE SERVICE
Management's Discussion & Analysis
Fiscal Year 2013

- Developed a Non-filers Identification Proofing and Authentication process for first-time filers for whom the IRS has no identification data using a combination of IRS and third party proofing, which standardized security services in Affordable Care Act applications and enhanced the ability to securely deliver services to customers via IRS.gov.

**Actions Planned or Underway for FY 2014 and Beyond:**

- Launch the third phase of the SSN Elimination project to mask SSNs on payment notices, beginning with four notices of installment agreements impacting an estimated 33 million notices annually.
- Upgrade technology to improve identity theft filters and taxpayer authentication procedures.

## 2. TAX COMPLIANCE INITIATIVES

**Summary of Major Issues:** Improve compliance and fairness in the application of the tax laws.

*Businesses and Individuals*

**Actions Taken:**

- Completed and posted on the web the final lesson for Virtual Small Business Tax Workshop (VSBTW) relating to "Hiring People Who Live in the U.S. but who aren't U.S. Citizens," which included closed captioning in English. These online workshops focus on providing taxpayers information to help them understand and meet their federal tax obligations.
- Updated tax information on IRS.gov in English and Spanish to help those recently released individuals in the inmate re-entry program with their taxes.
- Achieved 100% compliance from correctional agencies implementing IRS requirements for the annual prisoner data file required under newly enacted legislation.
- Developed a three-pronged approach to Improve Individual Tax Identification Number (ITIN) compliance by:
    - Manually reviewing returns involving new ITIN applications that claim Additional Child Tax Credit (ACTC) and/or American Opportunity Tax Credit (AOTC), if discrepancies are found, the returns are selected for audit.
    - Selecting ITIN returns that already have existing ITINs and appear to be claiming ACTC for potential audit.
    - Freezing potential refunds and auditing the returns of cases that meet the specific criteria.
- Identified over 1,000 amended returns using a new screening criteria for Form 1040X (Amended Income Tax Return) where ITIN filers increased the number of dependents and claimed additional ACTC/AOTC.
- Analyzed results from the FY 2012 and FY 2013 high dollar inventory with document matching issues and audited approximately 1,000 cases in an effort to combine AUR and audit issues.
- Tracked taxpayer transitions between CAP and CAP Maintenance and determined that due to unique situations, taxpayers transitioning from CAP to CAP Maintenance will be evaluated on a case-by-case basis.

30

**Actions Planned or Underway for FY 2014 and Beyond:**

- Conduct outreach efforts via direct contact and social media to market the Visual Small Business Tax Workshop (VSBTW) and establish relationships with organizations that represent small business owners in industries that frequently hire people who live in the U.S. but are not U.S. citizens.
- Proceed with SBTW translations for Chinese, Korean, Portuguese, Russian, Polish, French Creole, and Arabic.
- Implement closed captioning for new VSBTW for Spanish, Chinese, and Vietnamese.
- Collaborate with the state and federal correctional agencies to reduce and deter inmate tax fraud by signing agreements to exchange information.
- Identify tax preparers that continuously file egregious ITIN returns, resulting in identification and audit of certain returns that will support potential future prosecution efforts or penalty assertions.

*Tax-Exempt Entities*

**Actions Taken:**

- Completed three of the five remaining colleges and universities examinations and released the final report, making more than 180 adjustments to unrelated business income (UBI) that was reported for more than 30 different activities by colleges and universities.
- Revised the relevant IRM sections to provide guidance on promoter investigations in the tax-exempt arena.
- Issued 30-day report titled "Charting a Path Forward at the IRS: Initial Assessment and Plan of Action," outlining corrective actions to address TIGTA recommendations and other critical management challenges.
- Installed new leadership at all five levels of the senior executive managerial chain that had responsibility over the activities identified in the TIGTA report to ensure accountability.
- Led seven promoter investigations related to tax-exempt entities where retirement plans were accommodating parties to abusive transactions and where a promoter required a monetary donation to an associated charity for services rendered to individuals. Four retirement plans and three charitable organizations were involved in these abusive transactions.
- Coordinated with the Department of Justice (DOJ) to secure key records from its investigation of municipal bond bid-rigging, which are essential for the IRS to resume civil action on cases released by DOJ.
- Provided technical assistance to the DOJ in on-going criminal investigations of municipal bond bid-rigging, of which several defendants where sentenced and fined.
- Completed the Exempt Organizations Services and Assistance (EOSA) project, which allowed the IRS to better understand how small tax-exempt organizations receive tax-related information, determine their tax compliance responsibilities, and assess the most efficient and effective outreach methods to communicate with small and medium tax-exempt organizations.
- Supported the newly formed Security and Exchange Commission (SEC), Office of Municipal Securities, by meeting with officials to discuss market trends and observations, legislative and regulatory developments, compliance issues and projects,

31

and possible opportunities for additional collaboration pursuant to a memorandum of understanding between the IRS and SEC.

- o Created a Continued Professional Education (CPE) program for IRS personnel on securities regulation to help them better understand the relationship between tax and securities compliance.

- Completed 52 out of 54 remaining examinations of non-responders to the 401(k) questionnaire. Questionnaire data were collected through the examination process and incorporated into the 401(k) questionnaire project final report. The results of the final report revealed:
  - o 86% of plans use a pre-approved plan document.
  - o 96% of plans allow for catch-up contributions.
  - o 5% of plans included an automatic contribution arrangement.
  - o 68% of plans provide a matching contribution.
- Developed employee retirement plan examination projects based off of data from the 401(k) questionnaire project including a 100-case project on defaulted loans.
- Completed 163 out of 330 examinations of retirement plans detected through an advanced data mining application which compared past audit analytics to current return information in the Risk Modeling II project.
- Revised Forms 5300, 5310, and 5307 relating to applications for determination letters for qualified employee plans. The changes to the determination letter filing included eliminating elective demonstrations regarding coverage and nondiscrimination requirements and limiting the use of the Form 5307 to employers that have made limited modifications to a pre-approved volume submitter plan.
- Revised Revenue Procedure 2013-8 to allow the issuance of updated letters to sponsors of preapproved volume submitter plans, which are sample plans that will be adopted by at least 30 employer-clients that have name or address changes. In addition, the revision allows volume submitter practitioners to submit up to 10 trust documents with the basic document and an additional fee of $1,000 for each trust submitted in excess of 10, which made the rules consistent with the other type of preapproved plans.
- Issued Revenue Procedure 2012-50 allowing governmental plan sponsors to submit determination letter applications in multiple application cycles due to the unique issues these plans face in the process of securing approval for amendments.
- Suspended the use of "be on the lookout" (BOLO) lists in the application process for tax-exempt status.
- Added technical and programmatic experts to assist the Exempt Organizations staff with the review of applications for tax-exempt status.
- Created the new Emerging Issues Committee to provide expertise from other parts of the IRS to review screening and determination decisions.
- Completed development and training for the Emerging Issues Committee, which provides a process for Exempt Organizations determinations employees to elevate emerging issues for further technical evaluation and coordinated guidance and resolution.
- Collaborated with the Department of the Treasury to release the 2013-2014 Priority Guidance Plan, which includes guidance under §501(c)(4) relating to measurement of an organization's primary activity and whether it is operated primarily for the promotion of social welfare, and guidance relating to political campaign intervention.
- Developed a written procedure outlining the process for the Determinations Unit to formally request assistance from the Technical Unit and the Guidance Unit. The process enables the use of a spreadsheet-based tracking tool.

32

**Actions Planned or Underway for FY 2014 and Beyond:**

- Identify gaps and make improvements to the exempt organizations examination program.
- Initiate an unrelated business income (UBI) compliance project, to continue to address UBI tax gap issues for all exempt organizations.
- Issue guidance on how to measure the "primary activity" of IRC § 501(c)(4) social welfare organizations.
- Establish a robust Enterprise Risk Management Program.
- Conduct a comprehensive, agency-wide review of compliance selection criteria.
- Work with the National Taxpayer Advocate to increase taxpayers' awareness of mechanisms at their disposal for resolving issues with the IRS.
- Analyze examination results in the Risk Modeling II project of employee plans to determine the effectiveness of the selection methodology.
- Re-engineer the determination process for organizations seeking tax-exempt status and publish these procedures publicly.
- Evaluate the determination letter process for employee retirement plans to identify areas for improvement specifically related to alleviating the determination backlog and improving case processing times.
- Develop training or workshops to be held before each election cycle including, but not limited to, the proper ways to identify applications that require review of political campaign intervention activities.
- Develop guidance for specialists on how to process requests for tax-exempt status involving potentially significant political campaign intervention. This guidance will also be posted to the Internet to provide transparency to organizations on the application process.
- Develop training or workshops to be held before each election cycle including, but not limited to: a) what constitutes political campaign intervention versus general advocacy (including case examples) and b) the ability to refer for follow-up those organizations that may conduct activities in a future year which may cause them to lose their tax-exempt status.
- Provide oversight to ensure that potential political cases, some of which have been in process for three years, are approved or denied expeditiously.

*Tax Return Preparers*

**Actions Taken:**

- Issued corrective action letters to 4,200 professional credentialed (CPAs, Attorneys, and Enrolled Agents) return preparers in FY 2013 who were noncompliant due to nonpayment of a federal individual or business tax liability or the failure to file a required federal individual or business tax return, up from 500 in FY 2012. \
- Verified the personal tax compliance of approximately 920,000 registered PTIN holders, since program inception, and found that 97% were compliant. Monitored the tax obligations of the remaining 3% and treated the noncompliance based on program policy, which resulted in compliance from more than 2,200 return preparers.
- Developed risk models using National Research Program (NRP) data to select preparers for treatment tests.
- Implemented a study to compare the effectiveness of treatments for preparers who prepare inaccurate tax returns to improve return accuracy.

33

**Actions Planned or Underway for FY 2014 and Beyond:**

- Analyze results of the controlled study comparing the effectiveness of different treatments.

### 3. MODERNIZATION

**Summary of Major Issues:** Improve taxpayer service and efficiency of operations

**Actions Taken:**

- Transferred data from the CADE 2 database demonstrating the ability to feed data to downstream systems, which enabled robust data accuracy, a sustainable database system, and operational performance to facilitate future use.
- Released 45,395 square feet of available data center space by consolidating information technology operations in Atlanta, GA; Brookhaven, NY; Ogden, UT; Philadelphia, PA; and the Martinsburg and Memphis Enterprise Computing Centers to be used for other IRS space requirements.
- Delivered transcripts to third parties in seconds compared to days via electronic delivery to secure mailboxes using the Proof of Concept (PoC) application; however, the PoC was deactivated due to a low participation level of the Send My Transcript Proof of Concept, which also resulted in discontinuing plans to add more Income Verification Express Services (IVES) vendors and financial institutions.

**Actions Planned or Underway for FY 2014 and Beyond:**

- Deploy CADE 2 2014 Database Implementation to integrate testing and data assurance activities into the Annual Integrated Filing Season test.
- Convert the Martinsburg and Memphis Computing Centers into a new benchmarkable format, which integrates the best methods of data center strategy, planning, operation, and continuous improvement.
- Relocate Detroit Computing Center infrastructure and equipment to appropriate IRS facilities.

### 4. IMPLEMENTING THE AFFORDABLE CARE ACT AND OTHER TAX LAW CHANGES

**Summary of Major Issues:** Implement new tax provisions, including tax-related health care provisions of the Patient Protection and Affordable Care Act (ACA), and the American Recovery and Reinvestment Act (Recovery Act)

*Affordable Care Act (ACA)*

**Actions Taken:**

- Published *Healthcare Law Online Resources* (Pub. 5093), which provided internet resources available from IRS federal agency partners, including the Department of Health and Human Services (HHS), the Department of Labor and the Small Business Administration.
- Created a new ACA web page, which explains the tax benefits and responsibilities for individuals, families, and employers, as well as provides information regarding taxpayers' health insurance choices and how they may affect tax returns filed in 2015.

34

INTERNAL REVENUE SERVICE
Management's Discussion & Analysis
Fiscal Year 2013

- Launched two new IT services for Marketplace exchanges, providing both income and family size data and an optional computation service for exchanges to determine the maximum Advance Premium Tax Credit.
- Developed an ACA speaker's cadre that included speakers throughout the IRS who manage stakeholder outreach and education requests related to ACA tax law implementation during the 2013 Health Insurance Marketplace pre-enrollment and enrollment period.
- Conducted separate ACA discussions at an IRS Nationwide Tax Forum providing information on health care-related tax provisions for individuals and businesses, details about provisions that may affect taxpayers in 2013, and a preview of provisions beginning in 2014.
- Published 34 items of regulations and other guidance on ACA tax provisions including:
  - Proposed regulations on provision (1402), Net Investment Income Tax, and posted frequently asked questions on IRS.gov.
  - Final regulations on provision (6301), Patient-Centered Outcomes Research Trust Fund Fee (PCORTF), and a chart summary including questions and answers on IRS.gov.
  - Form 720, Quarterly Federal Excise Tax Return, was revised to provide for the reporting and payment of the PCORTF fee.
  - Proposed regulations on provision (9010), Health Insurance Providers Fee.
  - Proposed regulations on employer responsibility and information reporting by employers and insurers, and guidance providing transition rules for 2014.
- Completed the first three-year cycle of reviews of the community benefit activities of charitable hospitals, closing 1,141 reviews.
- Approved 19 applications received for recognition of tax-exempt status from Qualified Nonprofit Health Insurance Issuers (501(c) (29), CO-OP program participants).
- Closed 625 exempt organization examinations to determine eligibility for small business health care credits.
- Met with HHS and discussed the impact of the ACA provisions on Indian Tribal Governments, tribal employers, and tribal members and conducted 20 ACA outreach events focused on governmental entities, tax-exempt organizations, and Indian tribes.
- Conducted outreach activities across government agencies and stakeholder groups to ensure a coordinated communication on websites, phone scripts, and public events relating to:
  - Published guidance for Marketplace (Exchange) open season (Premium Tax Credit, exemptions from Individual Responsibility provision, and tax data disclosure rules).
  - Built, tested and deployed systems to support the Marketplace open season by providing income information from tax returns, and a computation tool for the advanced premium tax credit.
- Worked closely with HHS and the states on tax data safeguarding issues including education, correct and complete documentation, and on site validation reviews for:
  - HHS data services Hub.
  - Federally-Facilitated Marketplace.
  - State Marketplace, Medicaid and CHIP agencies.
- Completed documentation on the IRS/HHS computer matching agreement for the HHS data services Hub, and an approved safeguard procedures report for each recipient of tax data.
- Initiated a strategy to make online and self-service the desired method of delivery for ACA related contacts in order to:

35

      o  Minimize taxpayer burden.
      o  Ensure the IRS ACA strategy is aligned with peer-agencies' ACA strategies (e.g., HHS).
      o  Ensure optimization of IRS live resources by maintaining that the ACA scope is limited to addressing only tax-related inquiries.
- Collaborated with HHS, the Small Business Administration, and other partners to provide live and virtual outreach to individuals, employers, states, insurers, tax professionals, and other third parties.

**Actions Planned or Underway for FY 2014 and Beyond:**

- Complete development of an ACA awareness module, including key acronyms, for customer-facing managers and employees.
- Respond to requests to verify income and family size and requests to calculate the Advance Premium Tax Credit.
- Continue implementation of ACA mid-horizon provisions.
- Continue working with Federal and State agencies on implementation including outreach, guidance, information technology, and safeguarding of federal tax data.
- Continue preparing for Exchange-related tax provisions taking effect in 2014 and impacting 2015 filing season (customer service, IT systems and business processes, and compliance).
- Continue ACA outreach to stakeholders including individuals, employers, states, insurers, tax professionals, and other third parties.
- Coordinate new ACA IT requirements as modules are developed or enhanced.
- Ensure ACA requirements are met under e-Authorization Release 3 by aligning release schedules and supporting new modules as they are developed or enhanced.

*Other Tax Law Changes*

**Actions Taken:**

- Developed a prototype model for filing season 2014 that will identify Form 1120 corporate tax filings and freeze those who claim a fraudulent Fuel Tax credit.
- Selected 4,000 pilot cases involving information reporting on merchant payment cards. Mailed 1,000 notices for Third Party Network Merchant Card cases reported on a 1099-K (PayPal) and mailed 3,000 notices for General 1099-K for tax year 2011 cases that have unreported 1099-K information, and no Schedule C.
- Initiated implementation of the American Tax Relief Act (ATRA), which involved changing the tax rates, permanently fixing the Alternative Minimum Tax index for inflation, and returning the temporary 2% reduction in payroll taxes from 4.2% to 6.2%.
- Reviewed 1,200 active tax products to determine the impact of the ATRA legislation resulting in the initiation or revision of 630 tax products. More than 200 forms and instructions impacted by the legislation were posted by January 28, 2013, and 107 of 112 critical Individual filing season products were made available to the public on IRS.gov by January 30, 2013, the official start of the tax filing season.

**Actions Planned or Underway for FY 2014 and Beyond:**

- Implement Form 1120 corporate tax Fuel Tax Credit fraudulent prototype model to identify Form 1120 corporate tax filings and freeze those who claim a fraudulent Fuel Tax credit.

- Develop additional models to identify business filings claiming fraudulent Notice to Shareholder for Long Term Capital Gains and withholding claims that are either unsubstantiated or supported by fake or fraudulent information documents.
- Analyze additional business filings for other types of fraudulent refundable credits, such as the Accelerated Research Credit.
- Select, work, and monitor cases for Merchant Card and Security Cost Basis Reporting tests.
- Complete action plan and outreach efforts to implement the newly enacted American Taxpayer Relief Act (ATRA), Section 209 legislation.
- Determine impact of the Supreme Court of the United States' decision to invalidate the Defense of Marriage Act (DOMA) on employee plan programs and revise employee plan guidance as necessary.

## 5. FRAUDULENT CLAIMS AND IMPROPER PAYMENTS

**Summary of Major Issues:** Effective use of taxpayer funds

### Refundable Credits

**Actions Taken:**

- Identified multiple submission and processing issues regarding Form 8867 (Paid Preparer's Earned Income Credit Checklist) during filing season 2013, which required additional review of the TY 2012 returns to effectively and accurately identify the noncompliant returns:
  - Identified 2,500 Earned Income Tax Credit (EITC) paid preparers who submitted 2012 income tax returns without Form 8867.
  - Identified 66,000 tax returns that were submitted without Form 8867.
  - Developed an "early warning" strategy to address paid preparers who submit EITC returns missing Forms 8867 on the first occurrence.
- Stood up a new Automated Questionable Credit (AQC) operation, assembled two operational groups, and conducted multiple phases of training.
  - Created an automated tool to initiate taxpayer letters and input case resolution actions for all known AQC inventory.
  - Mailed 82,109 letters to taxpayers showing questionable income and/or credits reported on their tax returns.
- Selected 7,265 returns claiming children age 24 and over as disabled qualifying children (DQC) using pre-refund examination filters to address erroneous EITC claims.

**Actions Planned or Underway for FY 2014 and Beyond:**

- Analyze AQC case results and if warranted, recommend rule changes to improve selection criteria.

### Fraudulent Payments

**Actions Taken:**

- Initiated the Entity Fabrication Pilot focusing on taxpayers who used false information documents to claim fraudulent refunds.
- Updated the electronic fraud detection system to identify fabricated business entities with false Form W-2 filings as "suspicious."

37

- Conducted 368 audits for the Multi-DUPTIN audit program and coordinated with Submission Processing and other IRS offices to resolve processing of returns with questionable TINS for dependency exemptions.
- Suspended or rejected 6 million suspicious returns worth more than $13 billion in calendar year 2013.
- Implemented clustering filters to detect additional ID Theft cases with suspicious criteria, such as duplicate use of addresses and bank account information, resulting in over 392,000 returns selected and preventing approximately $1.2 billion in refunds.

**Actions Planned or Underway for FY 2014 and Beyond:**

- Refine filters, implement new codes, and finalize the treatment stream to identify fraudulent filings based on Entity Fabrication pilot results.
- Implement new programming, processes, and coding for false information documents.
- Develop and implement processes to mark or exclude false Forms W-2 from the automated verification process.

*Contract and Other Payments*

**Actions Taken:**

- Implemented processes and procedures requiring the inclusion of an overhead rate on reimbursable agreements, which:
  - Developed a customizable overhead worksheet enabling the IRS to use a consistent methodology, but to charge an overhead rate that is based on specific overhead services associated with the reimbursable agreement.
  - Communicated the requirement to charge an overhead rate through information sharing sessions and explained the new overhead procedures to customers.
  - Implemented a new process and criteria for the consideration of exemptions to avoid potential major impacts to business.
  - Collected an estimated $6 million in overhead costs.
- Established better controls regarding invoice payments, by requiring on-line training for Contracting Officer's Representatives, invoice approvers and their managers.
- Required all contract specialists and Federal Acquisition Certification for Contracting Officer Representatives enter training and certification data in the Federal Acquisition Institute Training Application System (FAITAS), which is verified quarterly.
- Reinforced controls over contract invoice review, approval, and payment processes, which:
  - Implemented a quarterly receipt and acceptance (R&A) review process to verify that end users maintained the proper R&A documentation required before making payment.
  - Evaluated supporting documentation to identify items that indicated noncompliance with policy and procedures, notifying organizations if significant errors were found.
  - Conducted training, made procedural changes, and other corrective actions to mitigate future instances of R&A errors.

**Actions Planned or Underway for FY 2014 and Beyond:**

- Develop and document an IRS-wide approach to identify, track, and monitor the adequacy of its acquisition workforce by forming teams that will:

38

INTERNAL REVENUE SERVICE
Management's Discussion & Analysis
Fiscal Year 2013

- o Define and communicate the definition of acquisition workforce throughout IRS and develop a method to track the acquisition workforce.
- o Identify and develop a strategy to collect data on current acquisition workforce efforts and employees, such as workload levels, attrition data, and employee skill gaps for workforce planning efforts.
- o Collect and analyze data to determine the number and skills of acquisition workforce personnel for a particular workload considering complexity and contract type.
- o Identify and implement a quality review process and controls to improve acquisition services.

## 6. PROVIDING QUALITY TAXPAYER SERVICE OPERATIONS

**Summary of Major Issues:** Improve taxpayer service

**Actions Taken:**

- Enhanced the MeF system, which successfully processed all Form 1040 electronic returns received within five minutes during non-peak periods and within two hours during peak periods.
- Completed the second and final phase of the TIN Matching re-engineering effort to resolve system integration, capacity, and maintenance issues, which resulted in fewer maintenance and delivery issues and reduced downtime.
- Promoted the benefits of alternate service delivery through the Facilitated Self Assistance (FSA) and Virtual Volunteer Income Tax Assistance (VITA) models to key partner groups, which contributed to a major increase in returns filed.
    - o Increased Facilitated Self Assistance (FSA) sites from 505 in FY 2012 to 942 in FY 2013, resulting in over 82,000 FSA federal returns compared to 15,000 in FY 2012.
    - o Created a new FSA Remote Model, which provided assistance through five toll-free call center staffed by Stakeholder Partnerships, Education and Communication (SPEC) partners at no cost to the IRS.
    - o Prepared over 60,000 returns at the 330 VITA sites offering the FSA Remote Model, representing 74% of the total FSA returns prepared.
    - o Increased Virtual VITA sites from 9 in FY 2012 to 34 in FY 2013 and prepared over 28,000 Virtual VITA returns compared to 4,020 in FY 2012.
    - o Surpassed the 2013 Alternative Filing Strategy goal of 100,000 returns by processing over 104,000.
    - o Deployed Virtual Service Delivery (VSD) in 14 new Taxpayer Assistance Centers (TAC) locations for walk-in customers.
- Tested VSD technology with taxpayers in pilot sites and determined that virtual face-to-face (VFTF) conferences could be held successfully between employees and taxpayers.
- Launched IRS2Go V3, a new version of the IRS2Go Smartphone application, which provided the application in Spanish for the first time and included minor updates to existing functionality. IRS2Go is available for both iOS and Android devices and has been downloaded by over 2.5 million users.

**Actions Planned or Underway for FY 2014 and Beyond:**

- Leverage new and existing partners to provide taxpayers expanded access via alternate filing methods such as FSA and virtual VITA.

39

- Evaluate capacity data to determine options to optimize VSD in support sites and identify locations for expansion.
- Implement VSD technology as a permanent part of campus operations.

## 7. HUMAN CAPITAL

**Summary of Major Issues:** Enable the IRS to achieve its mission

**Actions Taken:**

- Implemented the Entrance on Duty (EOD) System 2, which reduced administrative burden on the new hires and HR Staff by automating the collection of a numerous prescreening and onboarding forms.
- Transitioned the responsibility for adjudicating background investigations of appointees to the Personnel Security Office. Received 167 cases for adjudication of which 119 have been closed.
- Retired the IRS Career Opportunities Listing (COL). Jobs are now posted using the government wide system, USAJOBS/Career Connector, which supports the Presidential Hiring Reform and Hiring Excellence initiatives.
- Implemented use of the electronic Optional Form 306, Declaration for Federal Employment, which enabled the Automated Background Investigation System to automatically close an investigation without issues.
- Implemented the Management Selection Program (MSP) 2.0, which ensures the best qualified applicants possess the necessary skill sets to successfully perform in the position by integrating leadership succession readiness, technical competencies, and exceptional accomplishments into the process.
- Promoted career planning using the Leadership Succession Review (LSR) and Treasury Competency Assessment Process (TCAP) programs to expose IRS employees to other careers within the agency.
- Increased virtual recruitment efforts such as implementing the Schedule A disability portal for applicants applying for positions under the disability hiring authority initiative.
- Emphasized the recruitment of veterans and persons with disabilities:
  - Established and posted the Disability, Schedule A, and Veteran Plans that outline goals, objectives, resources, tools, and support available to managers.
  - Promoted the use of Veteran Hiring Authorities through IRS-wide communications.
  - Marketed the Treasury Veterans' Newsletter.
  - Launched a marketing campaign, called Veterans Employment Month, highlighting veterans' accomplishments, which resulted in an increase of 1000 unique hits to the IRS Careers veteran hiring website.
  - Expanded CareerConnector to improve hiring and to track applicant and workforce data.

**Actions Planned or Underway for FY 2014 and Beyond:**

- Develop and publish an employee recognition handbook.
- Complete online mandatory "back to basics" training by all employees to reinforce core values and assist them when confronted with issues and concerns.

40

INTERNAL REVENUE SERVICE
Management's Discussion & Analysis
Fiscal Year 2013

## 8. GLOBILIZATION

**Summary of Major Issues:** Increase the outreach efforts to foreign governments on cross-border transactions

**Actions Taken:**

- Partnered with the Department of the Treasury's Office of Terrorist Financing and Financial Crimes (TFFC) to address global money laundering.
- Joined the Treasury's Working Group on Terrorist Financing and Charities, an interagency working group that reviews the abuse of the charitable sector for the diversion of funds for the financing of terrorist activities.
- Developed bi-lateral working initiatives with the Department of the Treasury's TFFC Office aimed at identifying and addressing threats presented by all forms of illicit finance to the international financial system.
- Collaborated with the Treasury Executive Office for Asset Forfeiture (TEOAF) on the emerging issue of Third-Party Money Launderers (3PML) involved in domestic and global money laundering.
- Collected $5.5 billion in back taxes, interest, and penalties from 38,000 taxpayers by implementing strategic enforcement efforts and the offshore voluntary disclosure programs, which since inception, gave U.S. taxpayers with undisclosed offshore assets or income an opportunity to become compliant with the U.S. tax system and avoid potential criminal charges.
- Began implementing the Foreign Account Tax Compliance Act (FATCA) by conferring with more than 80 countries to gathering information about foreign accounts held by U.S. taxpayers via Tax Information Exchange Agreements (TIEAs):
  - Signed Model 1 Agreements, Agreement to Improve International Tax Compliance and to Implement FATCA, with seven countries: Denmark, Ireland, Germany, Mexico, Norway, Spain, and the United Kingdom.
  - Signed two Model 2 Agreements, Agreement for Cooperation to Facilitate the Implementation of FATCA, with two countries: Japan and Switzerland.
- Updated and provided guidance to taxpayers and stakeholders, through phone forums and other outreach events, about the Central Withholding Agreement (CWA) process of income reporting and tax payment requirements. A CWA is an agreement entered into by the non-resident alien (NRA) athlete or entertainer, a designated withholding agent, and the Internal Revenue Service. The agreement is for a specific tour or series of events and withholding is based upon the budget provided and net profits estimated. The new process requires CWAs are received by the IRS at least 45 days prior to the first event or would be subject to withholding at 30% of the gross income.

**Actions Planned or Underway for FY 2014 and Beyond:**

- Collaborate with the Department of Treasury's working group on Terrorist Financing and Charities to revise guidance.
- Enhance the case management system to identify the initiation and completion of criminal investigations of global money laundering schemes that are used by third party money launderers.
- Initiate criminal investigations of third party money launderers involved in domestic and global money laundering schemes.
- Develop technology and processes to implement Foreign Account Tax Compliance Act (FATCA) such as:

41

        o  FATCA Foreign Financial Registration website.

        o  International Data Exchange Service (IDES) for exchanging FATCA data with foreign financial institutions and foreign governments.

        o  International Compliance Management Model (ICMM) that will modernize Form 1042-S processes; receive, process, and store FATCA data; and make it accessible and usable for compliance analytics and caseload selection.

- Continue FATCA implementation by signing Intergovernmental Agreements to exchange tax information with additional countries.

## 9. TAXPAYER PROTECTION AND RIGHTS

**Summary of Major Issues:** Apply the tax laws fairly

**Actions Taken:**

- Increased the staff dedicated to refund fraud prevention and assisting taxpayers victimized by identity theft to 3,000 employees, more than twice the number in FY 2012.
- Trained 35,000 employees to detect the characteristics of identity theft cases and assist taxpayers who are victims of identity theft.
- Worked with victims to resolve and close more than 565,000 ID theft cases.
- Engaged federal and state agencies to participate in an identity theft data exchange to address identity theft and refund fraud. Began transmission of the data to two participating states, California and New York, resulting in sharing over 575,000 records of identity theft victims.
- Prevented fraudulent refunds of over $3.3 million as the result of referrals through the State Suspicious Filer Group, which consists of 41 participating states. Eight of the 41 participating states submitted information on over 5,000 suspicious filers under an exchange of information agreement.
- Launched the Law Enforcement Assistance Program (LEAP) nationwide. The program allowed victimized taxpayers to sign a waiver (Form 8821-A) authorizing the release of any tax information to the designated state or local law enforcement official pursuing the investigation. In FY 2013, 270 state/local law enforcement agencies from 31 states participated in the program, resulting in over 3,200 waiver requests for taxpayer consent access to their tax return data.
- Implemented new identity theft screening filters, including filters that target multiple refunds deposited into a single bank account or sent to a single address, to improve the ability to identify fraudulent returns before processing and issuing refunds.
- Improved customer service using the Two Dimension (2D) Barcode technology, which enabled assistors to instantly access the correct taxpayer account information and reduced notice processing errors.
- Initiated 1,492 identity theft investigations and recommended 1,257 cases for prosecution in FY 2013.

**Actions Planned or Underway for FY 2014 and Beyond:**

- Expand partnerships and participation in data exchange and information sharing programs to combat identity theft and tax fraud.
- Receive installment payment information through the 2D Barcode technology to expedite payment processing and reduce payment errors.

42

INTERNAL REVENUE SERVICE
Management's Discussion & Analysis
Fiscal Year 2013

## 10. ACHIEVING PROGRAM EFFICIENCIES AND COST SAVINGS

**Summary of Major Issues:** Use resources to focus on producing the best value for stakeholders

**Actions Taken:**

- Completed space reductions that resulted in the release of 557,000 square feet for an annualized rent savings of $15.7 million.
- Operated under an exception-only hiring freeze since December 2010 and reduced the total number of full-time, permanent IRS employees by almost 9,000.
- Secured buyout authority that resulted in the elimination of 1,224 positions.
- Limited employee travel and training to mission-critical projects, reducing training costs by 83 percent and training-related travel costs by 87 percent since 2010.
- Reduced spending on professional and technical service contracts by $200 million.
- Generated $60 million in printing and postage savings.
- Reduced retention allowances paid to senior staff.
- Updated and expanded the use of cost accounting information for exam and collections operations to improve program efficiency.
  - Expanded study on source of assessment for notices and added full time equivalents (FTE's) to the notice cost model to compare Balance Due notice process against other collection processes.
  - Developed the average hourly rate for use in determining the costs of different types of exams based on the hours expended on them.
  - Enhanced the cost/benefit study on notices to include costs and revenues for first through fourth balance due notices.
  - Developed the cost/benefit of the Federal Agency Delinquency program which established the threshold amount for write-off of aged delinquent accounts.
  - Developed the cost of examinations of tax-exempt organizations.
- Submitted requirements for the Return Review Program to design a web-based portal to exchange data between the IRS and correctional agencies that are required to submit inmate data to the IRS to speed up the process of receiving, reviewing, and loading data files into the system.

**Actions Planned or Underway for FY 2014 and Beyond:**

- Complete the development of the cost of collection processes by activity.
- Enhance the hourly rate for small business exams by incorporating more detail such as grade and activity type.
- Implement a formal process for distributing updated cost/benefit analyses.
- Support the development of a marginal revenue/cost model for exam by completing the costs of enforcement labor costs by job series and grade.
- Create a database to import prisoner/prison data files, which will eliminate any missing corrected files that are returned from the states.
- Use available data systems to systemically research missing prisoner Social Security Numbers that were not provided by the prisons.

43

INTERNAL REVENUE SERVICE
Management's Discussion & Analysis
Fiscal Year 2013

# FINANCIAL HIGHLIGHTS

## Revenue and Refund Trend Information

FY 2013 revenue receipts collected by IRS increased to $2.9 trillion. Federal tax revenues are collected through six major classifications: individual income and FICA/SECA, corporate income, excise taxes, estate and gift taxes, railroad retirement, and federal unemployment taxes.

FY 2013 tax refund activity totaled $364 billion, representing a decrease of approximately 2% from FY 2012. Federal tax refunds include refunds of tax overpayments, payments for interest, and disbursements for refundable tax credits such as Earned Income Tax Credit and the Additional Child Tax Credit.

## Excise Tax Trust Fund

The Quarterly Federal Excise Tax Return, Form 720, reports taxpayer liability for excise taxes. Taxpayers make periodic deposits in advance of filing the return. These deposits are classified as Federal Excise Tax. After the IRS receives and processes the returns, the IRS certifies amounts for several trust

|  | Liability Quarter Ended | |
|---|---|---|
|  | December 2010 – September 2011 | December 2011 – September 2012 |
| **Airport & Airway Trust Fund** | $11,511,789,465 | $12,524,925,643 |
| **Black Lung Disability Trust Fund** | $623,656,611 | $588,614,775 |
| **Highway Trust Fund** | $36,441,044,666 | $33,632,948,411 |
| **Total** | **$48,576,490,742** | **$46,746,488,829** |

funds. Amounts reported on the Statement of Custodial Activity are for fiscal year collections (October 1 through September 30). Because Form 720 reporting requirements are completed after receipt of most of the deposits, the certification amounts will not match the amounts collected in the fiscal year. The table shows revised receipts certified to the Airport and Airway Trust Fund, Black Lung Disability Trust Fund, and the Highway Trust Fund for the eight liability quarters from December 2010 through September 2012. The Department of the Treasury prepares the warrants and allocations to the trust funds.

## Analysis of Unpaid Assessments – Most Unpaid Assessments Are Not Receivables and Are Largely Uncollectible

The unpaid assessment balance includes amounts owed by taxpayers who file returns without sufficient payment as well as amounts assessed through the IRS enforcement programs. As reflected in the supplemental information to the IRS FY 2013 Financial Statements, the unpaid assessment balance was $374 billion as of September 30, 2013, and $199 billion (53%) of this balance consists of interest and penalties. Furthermore, the total outstanding balance of IRS unpaid assessments is largely uncollectible because it is composed mostly of compliance assessments and write-offs. Under federal accounting standards, unpaid assessments require taxpayer or court agreement to be considered federal taxes receivable. Assessments not agreed to by taxpayers or the courts are considered compliance assessments and are not considered federal taxes receivable. Assessments considered to have no future collection potential are called write-offs. The following provides detail on unpaid assessments:

44

- Taxes receivable represent $159 billion (43%) of unpaid assessments and increased $7 billion (5%) from $152 billion as of September 30, 2013. About $124 billion (78%) of this balance is estimated to be uncollectible due primarily because of the economic situations of the taxpayers. Except generally for bankruptcy situations, the IRS may continue collection actions for 10 years after the assessment. About $35 billion (22%) of taxes receivable is estimated to be collectible.

- Compliance assessments of $85 billion represent amounts that have not been agreed to by either the taxpayer or a court. These assessments result primarily from various IRS enforcement programs promoting voluntary compliance.

- Write-off amounts of $130 billion include amounts owed by defunct corporations with no assets and failed financial institutions. The remaining amounts are owed by taxpayers with extreme economic and/or financial hardships, deceased taxpayers, and taxpayers who are insolvent due to bankruptcy.

**The Integrated Financial System (IFS)**

The IFS is the financial management system for the administrative activities in IRS. IFS also provides timely financial statements and reports in accordance with the federal accounting and reporting standards including information for budgeting, analysis, and government-wide reporting.

In addition, IFS provides the core processes of General Ledger, Accounts Payable, Accounts Receivable, Budget Execution, Cost Accounting, Administrative Tax and Travel Accounting, Cost Allocations, some tax processing functionality for Health Coverage Tax Credit (HCTC) payments, Budget Formulation, Labor Forecasting and Budget Execution decision support.

INTERNAL REVENUE SERVICE
Management's Discussion & Analysis
Fiscal Year 2013

**Appendix A**

## Performance Measures Descriptions

| Goal 1: Improve Service to Make Voluntary Compliance Easier | |
|---|---|
| **Customer Service Representative (CSR) Level of Service** | The number of toll free callers that either speak to a Customer Service Representative or receive automated informational messages divided by the total number of attempted calls. |
| **Customer Contacts Resolved per Staff Year** | The number of Customer Contacts resolved in relation to time expended. |
| **Customer Accuracy – Tax Law Phones** | The percentage of correct tax law answers given by a live assistor on Toll-free tax law inquiries. |
| **Customer Accuracy – Customer Accounts (Phones)** | The percentage of correct account answers given by a live assistor on Toll-free account inquiries. |
| **Timeliness of Critical Individual Filing Season Tax Products to the Public** | The percentage of critical individual filing season tax products (tax forms, schedules, instructions, publications, tax packages, and certain notices required by a large number of filers to prepare a complete and accurate tax return) available to the public in a timely fashion. |
| **Timeliness of Critical TE/GE & Business Tax Products to the Public** | The percentage of critical other tax products, paper and electronic, available to the public in a timely fashion. |
| **Percent Individual Returns Processed Electronically** | The number of electronically filed individual tax returns divided by the total individual returns filed. |
| **Cost per Taxpayer Served ($) (HCTC)** | The costs associated with serving the taxpayers including program kit correspondence, registration, and program participation. |
| **Sign-Up Time (Days) – Customer Engagement (HCTC)** | The length of time between the first Program Kit mailing and the first payment received. |
| **Percent Business Returns Processed Electronically** | The percentage of electronically filed business tax returns divided by the total business tax returns filed. |
| **Refund Timeliness – Individual (Paper)** | The percentage of refunds resulting from processing Individual Master File paper returns issued within 40 days or less. |
| **Taxpayer Self Assistance Rate** | The percentage of taxpayer assistance requests resolved using self-assisted automated services. |
| Goal 2: Enforce the Law to Ensure Everyone Meets Their Obligation to Pay Taxes | |
| **Examination Coverage – Individual (1040)** | The sum of all individual 1040 returns closed by SB/SE, W&I, TEGE and LB&I (Field Exam and Correspondence Exam programs) divided by the total Full-Time Equivalent (FTE) expended in relation to those individual returns. |
| **Field Examination National Quality Review Score** | The score awarded to a reviewed field examination case by a Quality Reviewer using the National Quality Review System quality attributes. |
| **Office Examination National Quality Review Score** | The score awarded to a reviewed office examination case by a Quality Reviewer using the National Quality Review System quality attributes. |
| **Examination Quality – Large Business** | Average of the scores of the Large Business Return (LBR) cases reviewed by LB&I Quality Measurement System (LQMS). Case scores are based on the percentage of elements passed within each of the four auditing standard. |
| **Examination Coverage – Business (assets >$10M)** | The number of LB&I returns (C and S Corporations with assets over $10 million and all partnerships) examined and closed by LB&I during the current fiscal year divided by the number of filings for the preceding calendar year. |
| **Examination Efficiency – Individual (1040)** | The total number of SB/SE, W&I, LB&I and TEGE contact closures (a closure resulting from a case where IRS made contact) divided by the total FTE, including overtime. |

46

INTERNAL REVENUE SERVICE
Management's Discussion & Analysis
Fiscal Year 2013

Appendix A

## Performance Measures Descriptions (Continued)

| Goal 2: Enforce the Law to Ensure Everyone Meets Their Obligation to Pay Taxes (Continued) | |
|---|---|
| Automated Underreporter (AUR) Efficiency | The total number of SB/SE and W&I contact closures (a closure resulting from a case where IRS made contact) divided by the total FTE, including overtime. |
| Automated Underreporter (AUR) Coverage | The percentage representing the total number of SB/SE and W&I contact closures (a closure resulting from a case where IRS made contact) divided by the total return filings for the prior year. |
| Collection Coverage – Units | The volume of collection work disposed compared to the volume of collection work available. |
| Collection Efficiency – Units | The volume of collection work disposed divided by total collection FTE. |
| Field Collection National Quality Review Score | The score awarded to a reviewed collection case by a Quality Reviewer using the NQRS embedded quality attributes. |
| Automated Collection System (ACS) Accuracy | The percent of taxpayers who receive the correct answer to their ACS question. |
| Criminal Investigations Completed | The total number of subject criminal investigations completed during the fiscal year, including those that resulted in prosecution recommendations to the Department of Justice as well as those discontinued due to a lack of prosecution potential. |
| Number of Convictions | The number of criminal convictions. |
| Conviction Rate | The percent of adjudicated criminal cases that result in convictions. |
| Conviction Efficiency Rate ($) | The cost of Criminal Investigation's (CI) program divided by the number of convictions. |
| TE/GE Determination Case Closures | The number of cases closed in the Employee Plans or Exempt Organizations Determination programs, regardless of type of case or type of closing. |
| Strategic Foundations: Invest for High Performance | |
| Percent of Major BSM Projects within +/- 10% Cost Variance | The percentage of Major BSM projects that are within the +/- 10% threshold for cost. The cost variance is measured from the initial cost estimate versus current cost estimate. |
| Percent of Major BSM Projects within +/- 10% Schedule Variance | The percentage of Major BSM projects that are within the +/- 10% threshold for schedule. The schedule variance is measured from the initial schedule estimate versus current schedule estimate. |

47

INTERNAL REVENUE SERVICE
Management's Discussion & Analysis
Fiscal Year 2013

**Appendix B**

## Performance Management Data

| | 2010 | 2011 | 2012 | 2013 Target | 2013 Actual |
|---|---|---|---|---|---|
| **Goal 1: Improve Service to Make Voluntary Compliance Easier** | | | | | |
| Customer Service Representative (CSR) Level of Service | 74.0% | 70.1% | 67.6% | 70.0% | 60.5% |
| Customer Contacts Resolved per Staff Year | 10,744 | 12,419 | 16,320 | 16,754 | 20,767 |
| Customer Accuracy – Tax Law Phones | 92.7% | 93.4% | 93.2% | 93.0% | 95.7% |
| Customer Accuracy – Customer Accounts (Phones) | 95.7% | 98.0% | 95.6% | 95.0% | 96.0% |
| Timeliness of Critical Filing Season Tax Products to the Public | 95.3% | 96.3% | 97.2% | 95.0% | 58.9% |
| Timeliness of Critical TE/GE and Business Tax Products to the Public | 97.7% | 96.4% | 94.5% | 95.0% | 83.6% |
| Percent Individual Returns Processed Electronically | 69.3% | 76.9% | 80.5% | 80.0% | 82.5% |
| Cost per Taxpayer Served ($) (HCTC) | $9.52 | $12.36 | $14.43 | $15.00 | $13.41 |
| Sign-Up Time (Days) – Customer Engagement (HCTC) | 124 | 117.0 | 116.0 | 125.0 | 125.2 |
| Percent Business Returns Processed Electronically | 25.5% | 31.8% | 36.7% | 38.0% | 40.2% |
| Refund Timeliness – Individual (Paper) | 96.1% | 99.4% | 99.7% | 98.0% | 99.0% |
| Taxpayer Self Assistance Rate | 64.4% | 70.1% | 78.5% | 80.0% | 83.3% |
| **Goal 2: Enforce the Law to Ensure Everyone Meets Their Obligation to Pay Taxes** | | | | | |
| Examination Coverage – Individual | 1.1% | 1.1% | 1.0% | 1.0% | 1.0% |
| Field Examination National Quality Review Score | 84.9% | 85.8% | 87.4% | 86.9% | 89.2% |
| Office Examination National Quality Review Score | 91.6% | 90.4% | 91.3% | 91.1% | 90.3% |
| Examination Quality – Large Business[1] | | | | Baseline | 92.0% |
| Examination Coverage – Business (assets >$10M) | 5.7% | 6.2% | 6.2% | 4.6% | 5.6% |
| Examination Efficiency – Individual (1040) | 140 | 139 | 142 | 145 | 142 |
| Automated Underreporter (AUR) Efficiency | 1,924 | 2,007 | 2,041 | 2,035 | 2,025 |
| Automated Underreporter (AUR) Coverage | 3.0% | 3.3% | 3.2% | 2.9% | 2.8% |
| Collection Coverage – Units | 50.1% | 50.0% | 48.1% | 46.4% | 47.0% |
| Collection Efficiency – Units | 1,822 | 1,952 | 1,997 | 2,049 | 2,057 |
| Field Collection National Quality Review Score | 80.6% | 80.3% | 80.4% | 80.4% | 81.4% |
| Automated Collection System (ACS) Accuracy | 95.9% | 94.9% | 94.7% | 94.5% | 94.4% |
| Criminal Investigations Completed | 4,325 | 4,697 | 4,937 | 4,350 | 5,557 |
| Number of Convictions | 2,184 | 2,350 | 2,634 | 2,400 | 3,311 |
| Conviction Rate | 90.2% | 92.7% | 93.0% | 92.0% | 93.1% |
| Conviction Efficiency Rate ($) | $324,776 | $310,029 | $270,511 | $285,000 | $211,048 |
| TE/GE Determination Case Closures | 105,247 | 91,205 | 87,000 | 62,473 | 65,877 |
| **Strategic Foundations: Invest for High Performance** | | | | | |
| Percent of BSM Projects within +/- 10% Cost Variance | 40.0% | 71.4% | 50.0% | 90.0% | 0% |
| Percent of BSM Projects within +/- 10% Schedule Variance | 100.0% | 100.0% | 100.0% | 90.0% | 83.3% |

[1]. As a result of program changes that occurred in the Large Business and International (LB&I) organization, starting in FY 2013, a new Examination Quality - Large Business measure will replace the two previous LB&I quality measures - Examination Quality - Industry and Coordinated Industry.

48

# Financial Statements

## Principal Financial Statements

The principal financial statements have been prepared to report the financial position and results of operations of the Internal Revenue Service, pursuant to the requirements of the *Chief Financial Officers Act of 1990* (P.L. 101-576), the *Government Management Reform Act of 1994* and the Office of Management and Budget Circular No. A-136, *Financial Reporting Requirements*. The responsibility for the integrity of the financial information included in these statements rests with the management of the IRS. The audit of the IRS principal financial statements was performed by the Government Accountability Office.

The IRS principal financial statements for fiscal years 2013 and 2012 are as follows:

- The **Balance Sheet** presents the assets, liabilities, and net position.

- The **Statement of Net Cost** presents the net cost of operations by program. It includes the gross costs less any exchange revenue earned from activities.

- The **Statement of Changes in Net Position** presents the change in net position resulting from the net cost of operations, budgetary financing sources other than exchange revenues, and other financing sources.

- The **Statement of Budgetary Resources** presents the budgetary resources; the status of those resources; the change in obligated balances during the year; and the budgetary authority and agency outlays. Additional detail by major budget accounts is available in the Required Supplementary Information section.

- The **Statement of Custodial Activity** presents the sources and disposition of non-exchange federal tax revenues collected and refunds disbursed.

**Internal Revenue Service**
**Balance Sheet**
**As of September 30, 2013 and 2012**

**(In Millions)**

| | | 2013 | | 2012 |
|---|---|---|---|---|
| **Assets** | | | | |
| Intragovernmental | | | | |
| Fund balance with Treasury (Note 2) | $ | 2,251 | $ | 2,589 |
| Due from Treasury (Note 6) | | 2,910 | | 3,252 |
| Other assets (Note 3) | | 33 | | 111 |
| Total intragovernmental | | 5,194 | | 5,952 |
| | | | | |
| Cash and other monetary assets (Notes 4, 6) | | 491 | | 500 |
| Federal taxes receivable, net (Notes 5, 6) | | 35,000 | | 39,000 |
| General property and equipment, net (Note 7) | | 1,464 | | 1,289 |
| Other assets (Note 3) | | 16 | | 19 |
| **Total assets** | $ | 42,165 | $ | 46,760 |
| | | | | |
| **Liabilities** | | | | |
| Intragovernmental | | | | |
| Due to Treasury (Note 5) | $ | 35,000 | $ | 39,000 |
| Other liabilities (Note 8) | | 160 | | 254 |
| Total intragovernmental | | 35,160 | | 39,254 |
| Federal tax refunds payable | | 2,910 | | 3,252 |
| Other liabilities (Note 8) | | 1,898 | | 2,121 |
| **Total liabilities** | | 39,968 | | 44,627 |
| **Net position** | | | | |
| Unexpended appropriations | | 1,402 | | 1,490 |
| Cumulative results of operations | | 795 | | 643 |
| **Total net position** | | 2,197 | | 2,133 |
| **Total liabilities and net position** | $ | 42,165 | $ | 46,760 |

*The accompanying notes are an integral part of these statements.*

2

**Internal Revenue Service**
**Statement of Net Cost**
**For the Years Ended September 30, 2013 and 2012**

**(In Millions)**

| | 2013 | | 2012 | |
|---|---:|---|---:|---|
| **Program** | | | | |
| **Taxpayer Assistance and Education** | | | | |
| Gross cost | $ | 607 | $ | 925 |
| Earned revenue | | (1) | | (9) |
| Net cost of program | | **606** | | **916** |
| **Filing and Account Services** | | | | |
| Gross cost | | 3,829 | | 3,571 |
| Earned revenue | | (113) | | (84) |
| Net cost of program | | **3,716** | | **3,487** |
| **Compliance** | | | | |
| Gross cost | | 8,196 | | 8,572 |
| Earned revenue | | (384) | | (390) |
| Net cost of program | | **7,812** | | **8,182** |
| **Administration of Tax Credit Programs** | | | | |
| Gross cost | | 169 | | 180 |
| Earned revenue | | - | | - |
| Net cost of program | | **169** | | **180** |
| **Net cost of operations (Note 11)** | $ | **12,303** | $ | **12,765** |

*The accompanying notes are an integral part of these statements*

3

**Internal Revenue Service**
**Statement of Changes in Net Position**
**For the Years Ended September 30, 2013 and 2012**

**(In Millions)**

| | 2013 | | 2012 | |
|---|---|---|---|---|
| | Cumulative Results of Operations | Unexpended Appropriations | Cumulative Results of Operations | Unexpended Appropriations |
| **Beginning balances** | $ 643 | $ 1,490 | $ 537 | $ 1,471 |
| **Budgetary financing sources** | | | | |
| Appropriations received | | 11,819 | | 11,818 |
| Transfers in/out without reimbursement | 16 | - | | - |
| Other adjustments | | (692) | | (98) |
| Appropriations used | 11,215 | (11,215) | 11,701 | (11,701) |
| **Other financing sources** | | | | |
| Imputed financing | 1,272 | | 1,191 | |
| Transfers in/out without reimbursement | - | | 30 | |
| Transfers to general fund | (48) | | (51) | |
| **Total financing sources** | 12,455 | (88) | 12,871 | 19 |
| **Net cost of operations** | (12,303) | | (12,765) | |
| **Net change** | 152 | (88) | 106 | 19 |
| **Ending balances** | $ 795 | $ 1,402 | $ 643 | $ 1,490 |

*The accompanying notes are an integral part of these statements.*

4

Internal Revenue Service
Statement of Budgetary Resources
For the Years Ended September 30, 2013 and 2012

(In Millions)

| | 2013 | 2012 |
|---|---|---|
| **Budgetary resources** | | |
| Unobligated balance, brought forward, October 1 | $ 983 | $ 890 |
| Recoveries of prior year unpaid obligations | 137 | 108 |
| Other changes in unobligated balance | (72) | (96) |
| Unobligated balance from prior year budget authority, net | 1,048 | 902 |
| Appropriations (discretionary and mandatory) | 11,555 | 12,168 |
| Spending authority from offsetting collections (discretionary and mandatory) | 121 | 141 |
| **Total budgetary resources** | $ 12,724 | $ 13,211 |
| **Status of budgetary resources** | | |
| Obligations incurred (Note 12) | $ 11,730 | $ 12,228 |
| Unobligated balance, end of year: | | |
| Apportioned | 635 | 598 |
| Exempt from apportionment | 7 | 7 |
| Unapportioned | 352 | 378 |
| Total unobligated balance, end of year | 994 | 983 |
| **Total budgetary resources** | $ 12,724 | $ 13,211 |
| **Change in obligated balance** | | |
| Unpaid obligations, brought forward, October 1 (gross) | $ 1,673 | $ 1,777 |
| Obligations incurred | 11,730 | 12,228 |
| Outlays (gross) | (11,970) | (12,224) |
| Recoveries of prior year unpaid obligations | (137) | (108) |
| Unpaid obligations, end of year (gross) | 1,296 | 1,673 |
| Uncollected payments, federal sources, brought forward, October 1 | (42) | (53) |
| Change in uncollected customer payments from federal sources | 11 | 11 |
| Uncollected payments, federal sources, end of year | (31) | (42) |
| Memorandum (non-add) entries: | | |
| Obligated balance, start of year | 1,631 | 1,724 |
| **Obligated balance, end of year, (net)** | $ 1,265 | $ 1,631 |
| **Budget authority and outlays, net** | | |
| Budget authority, gross (discretionary and mandatory) | $ 11,676 | $ 12,309 |
| Actual offsetting collections (discretionary and mandatory) | (132) | (152) |
| Change in uncollected customer payments from federal sources (discretionary) | 11 | 11 |
| **Budget authority, net (discretionary and mandatory)** | $ 11,555 | $ 12,168 |
| Outlays, gross (discretionary and mandatory) | $ 11,970 | $ 12,224 |
| Actual offsetting collections (discretionary and mandatory) | (132) | (152) |
| Outlays, net (discretionary and mandatory) | 11,838 | 12,072 |
| Distributed offsetting receipts | (333) | (297) |
| **Agency outlays, net (discretionary and mandatory)** | $ 11,505 | $ 11,775 |

*The accompanying notes are an integral part of these statements.*

5

**Internal Revenue Service**
**Statement of Custodial Activity**
**For the Years Ended September 30, 2013 and 2012**

**(In Billions)**

|  | | 2013 | | 2012 |
|---|---|---|---|---|
| **Revenue activity** | | | | |
| **Collections of federal tax revenue (Note 13)** | | | | |
| Individual income, FICA/SECA, and other | $ | 2,449 | $ | 2,160 |
| Corporate income | | 312 | | 282 |
| Excise | | 61 | | 56 |
| Estate and gift | | 20 | | 14 |
| Railroad retirement | | 5 | | 5 |
| Federal unemployment | | 8 | | 7 |
| **Total collections of federal tax revenue** | | 2,855 | | 2,524 |
| (Decrease)/Increase in federal taxes receivable, net | | (4) | | 4 |
| **Total federal tax revenue** | $ | 2,851 | $ | 2,528 |
| | | | | |
| | | | | |
| **Distribution of federal tax revenue to Treasury** | $ | 2,855 | $ | 2,524 |
| (Decrease)/Increase in amount due to Treasury | | (4) | | 4 |
| **Total disposition of federal tax revenue** | | 2,851 | | 2,528 |
| **Net federal revenue activity** | $ | - | $ | - |
| | | | | |
| | | | | |
| **Federal tax refund activity** | | | | |
| Total refunds of federal taxes (Note 14) | $ | 364 | $ | 373 |
| Appropriations used for refund of federal taxes | | (364) | | (373) |
| **Net federal tax refund activity** | $ | - | $ | - |

*The accompanying notes are an integral part of these statements.*

6

**INTERNAL REVENUE SERVICE**

Notes to the Financial Statements

For the Years Ended September 30, 2013 and 2012

Note 1.    **Summary of Significant Accounting Policies**

A.  Reporting Entity

The Internal Revenue Service (IRS), a bureau of the U.S. Department of the Treasury (Treasury), celebrated its 150-year anniversary in 2012. The IRS originated in 1862, when Congress established the Office of the Commissioner of the Internal Revenue. The IRS administers the nation's tax laws and annually collects over 90 percent of the revenues funding the Federal Government. Numerous organizational divisions and major programs within the IRS contribute to this achievement.

**Operating Divisions**

The IRS has four operating divisions:

- Wage and Investment provides customer support, submission processing, and compliance activities with respect to individuals with wage and investment income;
- Small Business and Self-Employed administers compliance activities for small businesses, self-employed individuals, and others with income from sources other than wages;
- Tax Exempt and Government Entities oversees and assists employee plans, tax exempt organizations, and government entities in complying with tax laws and regulations; and
- Large Business and International serves corporations, subchapter S corporations, and partnerships with assets greater than $10 million on complicated issues involving tax law and accounting principles, and conducts business in an expanding global environment.

**Functional Divisions**

Five functional divisions within the IRS provide enforcement services supporting both internal and external operations:

- Appeals
- Criminal Investigation
- Communications & Liaison
- Taxpayer Advocate Service
- Office of Chief Counsel

The National Taxpayer Advocate reports directly to Congress and the IRS Chief Counsel reports to the Secretary of the Treasury.

**Support Divisions**

Nine support divisions provide shared services support to all of the IRS organizations:

- Information Technology
- Agency-Wide Shared Services
- Stewardship
- Wage & Investment - Stewardship
- Executive Leadership and Direction
- Privacy, Governmental Liaison and Disclosure
- Human Capital Office
- Human Capital Office Corporate Programs
- Chief Financial Officer

**Major Programs**

The IRS has four major programs (further discussed in Note 1.J., Program Costs):

- Taxpayer Assistance and Education
- Filing and Account Services
- Compliance
- Administration of Tax Credit Programs

7

**INTERNAL REVENUE SERVICE**

Notes to the Financial Statements

For the Years Ended September 30, 2013 and 2012

**B. Basis of Accounting and Presentation**

The financial statements have been prepared from the accounting records of the IRS in conformity with accounting principles generally accepted in the United States and in accordance with the Office of Management and Budget (OMB) Circular No. A-136, *Financial Reporting Requirements*. Accounting principles generally accepted for federal entities are the standards prescribed by the Federal Accounting Standards Advisory Board, which is the official body for setting accounting standards of the Federal Government.

These comparative financial statements and related notes consist of the Balance Sheet, the Statement of Net Cost, the Statement of Changes in Net Position, the Statement of Budgetary Resources (SBR), and the Statement of Custodial Activity.

The accounting structure of federal agencies is designed to reflect both accrual and budgetary accounting transactions. Under the accrual method of accounting, revenues are recognized when earned and expenses are recognized when incurred, without regard to receipt or payment of cash. Budgetary accounting facilitates compliance with legal constraints and controls over the use of federal funds. The Statement of Custodial Activity is presented on the modified cash basis of accounting. Under this method, cash collections and transfers to Treasury are reported on a cash basis. The collections and transfers to Treasury are adjusted on the face of the statement for the net change in taxes receivable, producing modified cash basis balances.

Certain assets, liabilities, earned revenues, and costs have been classified as intragovernmental throughout the financial statements and notes. Intragovernmental is defined as transactions made between two reporting entities within the Federal Government.

**C. Fund Balance with Treasury**

The fund balance with Treasury is the aggregate of funds in the accounts of the IRS, primarily appropriated funds, from which the IRS is authorized to make expenditures and pay liabilities.

The status of fund balance with Treasury represents amounts obligated and unobligated. The obligated balances not yet disbursed represent the unpaid funds with budgetary obligations. Unobligated balances, available represent amounts in unexpired appropriations as of the end of the current fiscal year. Unobligated balances become available when apportioned by the OMB. Unobligated balances, unavailable represent amounts in expired appropriations and amounts not apportioned for obligation as of the end of the current fiscal year.

**D. Other Assets**

**Accounts receivable** consist of amounts due to the IRS from the public and from federal agencies. Accounts receivable are recorded and reimbursable revenues are recognized as the services are performed and costs are incurred. The allowance for uncollectible accounts is based on an annual review of groups of accounts by age for accounts receivable balances older than one year.

**Advances to government agencies** primarily represent funds paid to the Treasury Working Capital Fund (WCF). Centralized services funded through the WCF consist primarily of telecommunication

8

**INTERNAL REVENUE SERVICE**

Notes to the Financial Statements

For the Years Ended September 30, 2013 and 2012

services, payroll processing, security, and employee programs. Advances to the public are cash outlays for criminal investigations and employee travel. All current Treasury WCF activities and assets are being transferred into the Treasury Franchise Fund. This will be completed in FY 2014.

**Forfeited property** held for sale is acquired as a result of forfeiture proceedings or foreclosure sales to satisfy a tax liability. The Federal Tax Lien Revolving Fund, established in accordance with Title 26 United States Code, Section 7810, is used to redeem real property foreclosed upon by a holder of a lien. The IRS may sell the property, reimburse the revolving fund in an amount equal to the redemption, and apply the net proceeds to the outstanding tax obligation.

### E. Cash and Other Monetary Assets

Imprest funds are maintained by headquarters and field offices in commercial bank accounts. Other monetary assets consist primarily of offers-in-compromise, voluntary deposits received from taxpayers pending application of the funds to unpaid tax assessments, and seized monies pending the results of criminal investigations.

### F. Federal Taxes Receivable, Net and Due to Treasury

Federal taxes receivable, net, and the corresponding liability, due to Treasury, are not accrued until related tax returns are filed or assessments are made by the IRS and agreed to by either the taxpayer or the court. Accruals are made to reflect penalties and interest on taxes receivable through the balance sheet date.

Taxes receivable consist of unpaid assessments (taxes and associated penalties and interest) due from taxpayers. The existence of a receivable is supported by a taxpayer agreement, such as filing of a tax return without sufficient payment, or a court ruling in favor of the IRS. The allowance reflects an estimate of the portion of total taxes receivable deemed to be uncollectible.

Compliance assessments are unpaid assessments for which neither the taxpayer nor a court has affirmed the taxpayer owes to the Federal Government. Examples include assessments resulting from an IRS audit or examination in which the taxpayer does not agree with the results. Write-offs consist of unpaid assessments for which the IRS does not expect further collections due to factors such as taxpayers' bankruptcy, insolvency, or death. Compliance assessments and write-offs are not reported on the balance sheet. Statutory provisions require the accounts to be maintained until the statute for collection expires.

**Tax Assessments**
Under the Internal Revenue Code (26 USC) Section 6201, the Secretary of the Treasury is authorized and required to make inquiries, determinations, and assessments of all taxes imposed and accruing under any internal revenue law, which have not been duly paid including interest, additions to the tax, and assessable penalties. The Secretary has delegated this authority to the Commissioner of the IRS. Unpaid assessments result from taxpayers filing returns without sufficient payments and from the enforcement programs of the IRS, such as examination, under-reporter, substitute for return, and combined annual wage reporting.

9

# INTERNAL REVENUE SERVICE

Notes to the Financial Statements

For the Years Ended September 30, 2013 and 2012

## Abatements

Section 6404 of the Internal Revenue Code (26 USC) authorizes the Commissioner of the IRS to abate certain paid or unpaid portions of assessed taxes, interest, and penalties. Abatements occur for a number of reasons and are a standard part of the tax administration process.

Abatements may be allowed for qualifying corporations claiming net operating losses that create a credit when carried back and applied against a prior year's tax liability. Additionally, abatements can correct previous assessments from enforcement programs, eliminate taxes discharged in bankruptcy, reduce or eliminate taxes encompassed in offers-in-compromise, eliminate penalty assessments for reasonable cause, eliminate contested assessments caused by mathematical or clerical errors, and eliminate assessments contested after the liability has been satisfied. Abatements may result in claims for refunds or reductions of the unpaid assessed amounts.

## G. General Property and Equipment

General property and equipment is recorded at historical cost. It consists of tangible assets and software. The IRS depreciates property and equipment on a straight line basis over its estimated useful life. Except for leases meeting the 75 percent useful life and/or 90 percent of net present value (NPV) criteria, the IRS records a half-year of depreciation in the first year and the final year for all property and equipment. The IRS depreciates leases meeting the 75 percent useful life and/or 90 percent of NPV criteria over the life of the leases, with no use of a half-year convention. Disposals are recorded when deemed material.

The IRS capitalization policy for property and equipment by asset class and threshold:

| Asset Class | Capitalization Threshold |
|---|---|
| ADP equipment | Capitalized regardless of acquisition cost. However, mainframe and server components and related commercial off the shelf software purchased separately are only capitalized when the bulk cost is $50 thousand or greater. |
| Non-ADP equipment | Assets with bulk cost of $50 thousand or greater |
| Furniture | Capitalized regardless of acquisition cost |
| Investigative equipment | Assets with bulk cost of $50 thousand or greater |
| Vehicles | Capitalized regardless of acquisition cost |
| Major systems | Projects with costs of $20 million or greater |
| Internal Use Software | Major business systems modernization projects with an estimated cost of $10 million per year or $50 million over the life cycle. |
| Leasehold Improvements | Improvements with bulk cost of $50 thousand or greater |
| Assets under capital lease | Assets with bulk cost of $50 thousand or greater |

Major systems was a category for large-scale computer systems prior to Statement of Federal Financial Accounting Standards No. 10 (SFFAS No. 10), *Accounting for Internal Use Software.*

10

# INTERNAL REVENUE SERVICE

Notes to the Financial Statements

For the Years Ended September 30, 2013 and 2012

Internal Use Software captures the costs of major Business Systems Modernization (BSM) projects in accordance with SFFAS No. 10. It encompasses software design, development, and testing of projects adding significant new functionality and long-term benefits. Costs for developing internal use software are accumulated in work in process until final acceptance and testing are successfully completed. When the software is completed and placed into service, the costs are transferred to amortizable property.

## H. Federal Tax Refunds Payable and Due from Treasury

Federal tax refunds payable is comprised of measurable and legally payable amounts due to taxpayers under established refund processes of the IRS. It is a fully funded liability offset by a corresponding asset due from Treasury. The IRS records an amount due from Treasury to designate approved funding to pay year-end tax refund liabilities to taxpayers.

## I. Financing Sources and Revenues

### Appropriations Received

The IRS receives the majority of its funding through annual, multi-year, and no-year appropriations available for use within statutory limits for operating and capital expenditures. Appropriations are recognized as budgetary financing sources when the related expenses are incurred.

### Appropriations

The major budget accounts are:

- Taxpayer Services
- Enforcement
- Operations Support
- Other

**Taxpayer Services** provides funds for the direct costs of the Taxpayer Assistance and Education and the Filing and Account Services Programs discussed in Note 1. J., Program Costs.

**Enforcement** provides resources for the direct costs of the Compliance Program discussed in Note 1. J., Program Costs. Additionally, it funds the direct costs of administering the Earned Income Tax Credit Program (EITC).

**Operations Support** funds the indirect costs of all programs. Activities include executive planning and direction; shared service support for facilities, rent, utilities and security; procurement; printing; postage; headquarters' activities such as strategic planning, finance, human resources and Equal Employment Opportunity; research and statistics of income; and information systems, data processing and telecommunication.

**Other** includes BSM and Administrative Expenses, Recovery Act. The BSM appropriation provides resources for the planning and capital asset acquisition of information technology to modernize the business systems. Additionally, BSM is obligated pursuant to an expenditure plan submitted to Congress. Administrative Expenses, Recovery Act supports the funding for the administration of new and expanded tax credit programs of the *American Recovery and Reinvestment Act of 2009* (ARRA). In 2010, the IRS began administering various tax provisions included in the *Patient Protection and Affordable Care Act of 2010.*

11

## INTERNAL REVENUE SERVICE

Notes to the Financial Statements

For the Years Ended September 30, 2013 and 2012

**Exchange Revenues**

Exchange revenues recognized by the IRS represent reimbursements and user fees. Reimbursements are recognized as the result of costs incurred for services performed for federal agencies or the public under reimbursable agreements. User fees are derived from transactions with the public and are generally recognized when the fees are collected.

**Imputed Financing Sources**

Other financing sources include imputed financing sources to offset the imputed costs recognized for goods or services received from other federal agencies without reimbursement from the IRS. The imputed costs are pension and other benefit costs administered by the Office of Personnel Management (OPM), costs of processing payments and collections by the Bureau of Fiscal Service, cost of providing training by the Federal Law Enforcement Training Center, and legal judgments paid by the Treasury Judgment Fund.

**J. Program Costs**

**Taxpayer Assistance and Education** provides services to assist taxpayers with tax return preparation. Primary activities include tax law interpretations, developing and disseminating tax forms and publications, researching customer needs and establishing partnerships with stakeholder groups, and taxpayer advocacy. In addition, these programs continue to emphasize taxpayer education, outreach and enhancing prefiling taxpayer support through electronic media. Earned revenues include reimbursable revenues from services provided to other federal agencies.

**Filing and Account Services** provides resources and support services to taxpayers in filing returns or paying taxes, and for the issuance of refunds and maintenance of taxpayer accounts. Program activities include providing assistance, education and compliance services to taxpayers through telephone, correspondence and electronic means to resolve account and notice inquires. Earned revenues include user fees from photocopies, US Residency Certification and Income Verification Express Service, and reimbursable revenues from services provided to other federal agencies.

**Compliance** administers compliance activities after a return is filed to identify and correct possible errors or underpayments. This program includes examination and collection programs, which ensure proper payment and tax reporting; criminal investigation programs to uncover violations of internal revenue tax laws and other financial crimes; the development and printing of published IRS guidance materials; and support of taxpayers for pre-filing agreements, determination letters, and advance pricing agreements. It also includes specialty program examinations, international collections, and international examinations. Earned revenues are primarily from user fees for installment agreements, letter rulings and determinations, offers-in-compromise, enrollment programs and return preparer registrations, and reimbursable revenues from services provided to other federal agencies.

**Administration of Tax Credit Programs** administers primarily the EITC program, which works closely with internal and external stakeholders through expanded customer service and public outreach, enforcement, and research efforts to increase the number of eligible taxpayers who claim the EITC and to reduce the number of EITC claims paid in error. The EITC payments actually refunded to individuals or credited against tax liabilities are not included in program costs. This program also includes a portion of the costs related to administering the Health Coverage Tax Credit (HCTC). The HCTC program activities focus on providing staff, training, and direct support to administer the health

12

**INTERNAL REVENUE SERVICE**

Notes to the Financial Statements

For the Years Ended September 30, 2013 and 2012

insurance tax credit portion of the *Trade Adjustment Assistance Reform Act of 2002*. These costs do not encompass payments made to health insurance carriers on behalf of participants or tax credits refunded to qualifying individuals. In fiscal year 2012, HCTC program activity costs were moved under Filing and Account Services except for costs related to HCTC obligations made prior to fiscal year 2012, which are still reported here. This tax credit will no longer be available beginning January 1, 2014. (See Other Information - unaudited for discussion of refundable tax credits.)

### K. Custodial Activity

**Non-exchange Revenues**
The IRS collects custodial non-exchange revenues for taxes levied against taxpayers for: individual and corporate income, Federal Insurance Contributions Act (FICA) and Self-Employment Contribution Act (SECA), excise, estate, gift, railroad retirement, and federal unemployment taxes. These collections are not available to the IRS for obligation or expenditure and are recognized as custodial revenues when collected. The sources of federal tax revenue and their distribution to the general fund of the Treasury are reported on the Statement of Custodial Activity.

**Permanent Indefinite Appropriations**
The IRS was granted permanent and indefinite budgetary authority through legislation to disburse tax refund principal and related interest as they become due. The permanent and indefinite appropriations are not subject to budgetary ceilings set by Congress during the annual appropriation process.

Refunds due to taxpayers are reported as federal tax refunds payable on the Balance Sheet. The IRS records an offsetting asset, due from Treasury, to reflect the year-end budget authority to pay this liability.

Disbursements for tax refunds and related interest, reported on the Statement of Custodial Activity, are offset by appropriations used for refunds. Disbursements for refunds are not a cost to the IRS, but rather a cost to the Federal Government as a whole.

### L. Funds from Dedicated Collections

In accordance with SFFAS No. 43, *Funds from Dedicated Collections: Amending Statement of Federal Financial Accounting Standards 27, Identifying and Reporting Earmarked Funds*, Funds from Dedicated Collections are financed by specifically identified revenues, which remain available over time. These specifically identified revenues are required by statute to be used for designated activities, benefits or purposes and must be accounted for separately from the Federal Government's general revenues.

The Federal Tax Lien Revolving Fund (20X4413) was established pursuant to section 112(a) of the *Federal Tax Lien Act of 1966*, to serve as the source of financing for the redemption of real property by the United States.

The Private Collection Agent Program (20X5510) was established under the *American Jobs Creation Act of 2004*. In March 2009, the IRS Commissioner announced the program would not renew the contracts with the private debt collection agencies. Unobligated funds from prior year collection of delinquent federal tax liabilities have been retained by the IRS to fund ongoing enforcement activities.

13

## INTERNAL REVENUE SERVICE

Notes to the Financial Statements

For the Years Ended September 30, 2013 and 2012

### M. Allocation Transfers

The IRS is a party to allocation transfers from the Department of Transportation's (Transportation) Federal Highway Administration and the Department of Health and Human Services (HHS) as a receiving entity. Obligations and outlays incurred by the IRS are charged to the allocation account as it executes the delegated activity on behalf of Transportation and HHS. Financial activity for the allocation transfers are reported in the financial statements of Transportation and HHS.

### N. Fiduciary Activities

Fiduciary activities are the collection or receipt, and the management, protection, accounting, investment and disposition by the Federal Government of cash or other assets in which non-federal individuals or entities have an ownership interest the Federal Government must uphold.

The IRS fiduciary activities include the net collections for a taxable year from United States (U.S.) military and federal employees working in the U.S. territories of the Northern Mariana Islands, the U.S. Virgin Islands, Guam, and American Samoa. These fiduciary assets are not assets of the IRS.

### O. Employee Compensation and Benefits

#### Accrued Annual, Sick, and Other Leave

Annual and compensatory leave is expensed with an offsetting liability as it is earned, and the liability is reduced as leave is taken. Each year, the IRS adjusts the balance in the accrued annual leave liability account to reflect current pay rates. To the extent current or prior year appropriations are not available to fund annual and compensatory leave earned but not taken, funding is obtained from future financing sources. Sick leave and other types of non-vested leave are expensed as taken.

#### Federal Employees Compensation Act

The Federal Employees Compensation Act (FECA) provides income and medical cost protection to covered federal civilian employees injured on the job, to employees who have incurred work-related occupational diseases, and to beneficiaries of employees whose deaths were attributed to job-related injuries or occupational diseases. The FECA program is administered by the U.S. Department of Labor (DOL), which pays valid claims and subsequently seeks reimbursement for claims paid. Accrued FECA liability represents amounts due to the DOL for claims paid on behalf of the IRS. Actuarial FECA liability represents the liability for future workers' compensation benefits, which includes the expected liability for death, disability, medical, and miscellaneous costs for approved cases. The DOL estimates the liability for future payments as a result of past events.

#### Employee Pension Benefits

The IRS recognizes the full costs of its employees' pension benefits. The liabilities associated with these costs are reported by the OPM, who administers the plans. Eligibility of employees to participate in the Civil Service Retirement System (CSRS) or the Federal Employees Retirement System (FERS) is based on their hire date with the Federal Government, and the IRS contributes a percentage of an employee's basic pay toward the employee's retirement plan. The IRS contributions for CSRS were 7.0 percent for regular employees and 7.5 percent for law enforcement officers. For FERS, the IRS contributed 11.9 percent and 26.3 percent for regular employees and law enforcement officers, respectively, employed on December 31, 2012. Beginning January 1, 2013, the Revised Annuity Employees legislation increased new federal employees' contributions by 2.3 percent of

14

## INTERNAL REVENUE SERVICE

Notes to the Financial Statements

For the Years Ended September 30, 2013 and 2012

salary. The IRS contributed 9.6 percent for regular employees and 24 percent regular employees and law enforcement officers, respectively.

Employees covered by either CSRS or FERS are also eligible to contribute to the Thrift Savings Plan (TSP), a defined contribution plan. A TSP account is automatically established for employees participating in FERS, and the IRS makes a mandatory contribution to this plan equal to one percent of an employee's compensation. Additionally, the IRS matches up to four percent of the compensation for FERS-eligible employees contributing to their TSP. No TSP matching contributions are made for employees participating in the CSRS.

### Employee Health and Life Insurance Benefits

Employees are eligible to participate in the Federal Employees Health Benefit Program (FEHB) and Federal Employees Group Life Insurance Program (FEGLI). The FEHB offers a wide variety of group plans and coverage. The coverage is available to employees, retirees, and their eligible family members. The cost for each plan varies and is shared between the IRS and the employee. Employees participating in the FEGLI program can obtain basic term life insurance, with the employee paying two-thirds of the cost and the IRS paying one-third. Additional coverage is optional, to be paid fully by the employee. The basic life coverage may continue into retirement if certain requirements are met. The IRS recognizes the full cost of providing these benefits.

### P. Use of Estimates

The preparation of financial statements in conformity with accounting principles generally accepted in the United States of America requires management to make estimates and assumptions related to the reporting of assets, liabilities, revenues, and expenses, and the disclosure of contingent liabilities. Actual results could differ from those estimates.

### Q. Statement of Budgetary Resources

In accordance with OMB Circular No. A-136, *Financial Reporting Requirements*, the IRS updated the SBR presentation in the FY 2013 financial statements to better align with the new SF-133 Report on Budget Execution and Budgetary Resources. All fiscal year 2012 activity and balances reported on the SBR have been reclassified to conform to the presentation in the current year.

15

INTERNAL REVENUE SERVICE

Notes to the Financial Statements

For the Years Ended September 30, 2013 and 2012

### Note 2. Fund Balance with Treasury

| (In Millions) | | 2013 | | 2012 |
|---|---|---|---|---|
| General funds | $ | 1,919 | $ | 2,236 |
| Special funds | | 324 | | 364 |
| Revolving funds | | 7 | | 6 |
| Other funds | | 1 | | (17) |
| **Fund balance with Treasury** | **$** | **2,251** | **$** | **2,589** |

| (In Millions) | | 2013 | | 2012 |
|---|---|---|---|---|
| Unobligated balances: | | | | |
| Available | $ | 641 | $ | 605 |
| Unavailable | | 352 | | 378 |
| Obligated balance not yet disbursed | | 1,265 | | 1,631 |
| Non-budgetary FBWT | | (7) | | (25) |
| **Status of fund balance with Treasury** | **$** | **2,251** | **$** | **2,589** |

### Note 3. Other Assets

| (In Millions) | | 2013 | | | | 2012 | | |
|---|---|---|---|---|---|---|---|---|
| | | Intra-governmental | | With the Public | | Intra-governmental | | With the Public |
| Accounts receivable, net | $ | 18 | $ | 9 | $ | 23 | $ | 11 |
| Advances | | 15 | | 6 | | 68 | | 7 |
| Forfeited property held for sale | | - | | 1 | | - | | 1 |
| Clearing accounts | | - | | - | | 20 | | - |
| **Other assets** | **$** | **33** | **$** | **16** | **$** | **111** | **$** | **19** |

### Note 4. Cash and Other Monetary Assets

| (In Millions) | | 2013 | | 2012 |
|---|---|---|---|---|
| Imprest fund | $ | 7 | $ | 6 |
| Other monetary assets | | 484 | | 494 |
| **Cash and other monetary assets** | **$** | **491** | **$** | **500** |

16

## INTERNAL REVENUE SERVICE

Notes to the Financial Statements

For the Years Ended September 30, 2013 and 2012

**Note 5.    Federal Taxes Receivable, Net and Due to Treasury**

| (In Billions) | 2013 | 2012 |
|---|---|---|
| Federal taxes receivable | $    159 | $    152 |
| Allowance for uncollectible taxes receivable | (124) | (113) |
| **Federal taxes receivable, net and due to Treasury** | **$     35** | **$     39** |

Federal taxes receivable consists primarily of tax assessments, penalties, and interest not paid or abated, which were agreed to by the taxpayer and the IRS or upheld by the courts. The Allowance for uncollectible taxes receivable represents the difference between the gross Federal taxes receivable and the portion estimated to be collectible based on projections of collectability from a statistical sample of taxes receivable. Federal taxes receivable, net is the portion of gross Federal taxes receivable estimated to be collectible, and due to Treasury is the offsetting liability to be transferred to Treasury when collected. As of September 30, 2013, there is no federal tax receivable from uncollected Branded Prescription Drug fees. As of September 30, 2012, the Federal taxes receivable, net included $2 billion in uncollected Branded Prescription Drug fees.

**Note 6.    Non-entity Assets**

| (In Millions) | 2013 | | 2012 | |
|---|---|---|---|---|
| | Intra-governmental | With the Public | Intra-governmental | With the Public |
| Due from Treasury | $    2,910 | $         - | $    3,252 | $         - |
| Federal taxes receivable, net | - | 35,000 | - | 39,000 |
| Other monetary assets | - | 484 | - | 494 |
| **Non-entity assets** | **$    2,910** | **$  35,484** | **$    3,252** | **$  39,494** |

Non-entity assets are not available for use by the IRS. Federal taxes receivable are collected for the U.S. Government, but the IRS does not have the authority to spend them.

17

INTERNAL REVENUE SERVICE

Notes to the Financial Statements

For the Years Ended September 30, 2013 and 2012

Note 7.   **General Property and Equipment, Net**

| (In Millions) | Useful Life (Years) | Cost | Accumulated Depreciation | 2013 Net Book Value | 2012 Net Book Value |
|---|---|---|---|---|---|
| ADP assets | 3 to 7 | $ 1,362 | $ (910) | $ 452 | $ 481 |
| Internal use software | 2 to 15 | 1,218 | (758) | 460 | 455 |
| Leasehold improvements | 10 | 254 | (113) | 141 | 145 |
| Major systems | 7 | 221 | (221) | - | - |
| Internal use software – work in process | | 292 | - | 292 | 98 |
| Vehicles | 5 | 55 | (47) | 8 | 15 |
| Furniture and non-ADP equipment | 8 to 10 | 156 | (51) | 105 | 88 |
| Assets under capital lease | 7 | 9 | (3) | 6 | 6 |
| Investigative equipment | 10 | 5 | (5) | 0 | 1 |
| Property and equipment | | $ 3,572 | $ (2,108) | $ 1,464 | $ 1,289 |

The Cost column represents the historical cost of property and equipment, net of disposals. The cost basis for FY 2013 and FY 2012 is $3,572 million and $3,509 million, respectively. Accumulated depreciation for FY 2013 and FY 2012 is $2,108 million and $2,220 million, respectively.

The IRS has 17 internal use software projects, including deployed and work in process:
- Account Management Services (AMS) provides the applications to monitor and interface with taxpayers, issue enhanced notices, and deliver improved customer support and functionality.
- Affordable Care Act (ACA) is the development and implementation of systems to support IRS' tax administration responsibilities associated with the *Patient Protection and Affordable Care Act.*
- Customer Account Data Engine 2 (CADE 2) is leveraging existing systems and new development to implement a single data-centric solution, which provides daily processing of individual taxpayer accounts and establishes a solid data foundation for the future. CADE 2 replaced Current Customer Account Date Engine (CADE) in FY2012.
- Customer Communications is a customer service telephone system.
- Custodial Detail Database (CDDB), the subsidiary ledger for Redesign Revenue and Accounting System (RRACS), provides the functionality needed for custodial financial management and reporting.
- E-Services is a system of web-based products and services for tax practitioners and the public.
- Enterprise Systems Management (ESM) is an infrastructure system allowing remote monitoring and network management.
- Foreign Account Tax Compliance Act (FATCA) is being developed to enable foreign financial institutions to report information to the IRS about financial accounts held by U.S. taxpayers or foreign entities in which U.S. taxpayers hold a substantial ownership interest.
- Information Reporting and Document Matching (IRDM) is a business document matching program designed to increase voluntary compliance and accurate reporting of income through the use of third party information reporting data.
- Integrated Financial System (IFS) is the IRS administrative financial system.
- Integrated Procurement System (IPS) is the re-engineered procurement system meeting current enterprise architecture and security standards.

18

**INTERNAL REVENUE SERVICE**

Notes to the Financial Statements

For the Years Ended September 30, 2013 and 2012

The IRS has 17 internal use software projects, continued:

- Internet Refund Fact of Filing allows taxpayers to review the status of their refund.
- Knowledge Incident/Problem Service Asset Management (KISAM) is the IRS' asset and problem management system.
- Modernized e-file (MeF) is an electronic filing system for tax returns.
- RRACS adds enhancements to financial reporting of taxpayer receipts and adds traceability between summary records and the detailed subsidiary ledger (CDDB).
- Return Review Program (RRP) is an automated system designed to maximize fraud detection at the time tax returns are filed.
- Security and Technology Infrastructure Release (STIR) is the infrastructure for information technology security.

**Deployed Internal Use Software**

| (In Millions) | Cost | Accumulated Depreciation | 2013 Net Book Value | 2012 Net Book Value |
|---|---|---|---|---|
| MeF | $ 346 | $ (230) | $ 116 | $ 115 |
| CADE 2 | 258 | (55) | 203 | 241 |
| IFS | 167 | (148) | 19 | - |
| E-Services | 141 | (141) | - | - |
| AMS | 78 | (24) | 54 | 60 |
| STIR | 76 | (76) | - | - |
| IRDM | 59 | (9) | 50 | 26 |
| Customer Communications | 25 | (25) | - | |
| ESM | 16 | (16) | - | - |
| Internet Refund Fact of Filing | 15 | (15) | - | - |
| CDDB | 8 | (6) | 2 | 3 |
| IPS | 8 | - | 8 | - |
| KISAM | 7 | (3) | 4 | 5 |
| RRACS | 7 | (3) | 4 | 5 |
| Other | 7 | (7) | - | - |
| Deployed internal use software | $ 1,218 | $ (758) | $ 460 | $ 455 |

**Work in Process Internal Use Software**

| (In Millions) | 2013 | 2012 |
|---|---|---|
| ACA | $ 182 | $ - |
| RRP | 65 | 26 |
| MeF | 24 | 13 |
| FATCA | 21 | 10 |
| IRDM | - | 24 |
| IFS Update | - | 17 |
| IPS | - | 8 |
| Work in process internal use software | $ 292 | $ 98 |

19

**INTERNAL REVENUE SERVICE**

Notes to the Financial Statements

For the Years Ended September 30, 2013 and 2012

**Note 8.   Liabilities**

**Other Liabilities**

| (In Millions) | | 2013 | | | | |
|---|---|---|---|---|---|---|
| | | Current | | Non-Current | | Total |
| **Intragovernmental:** | | | | | | |
| Accrued payroll and benefits | $ | 47 | $ | - | $ | 47 |
| Accrued FECA liability | | 45 | | 54 | | 99 |
| Accrued expense | | 14 | | - | | 14 |
| **Other liabilities** | **$** | **106** | **$** | **54** | **$** | **160** |
| | | | | | | |
| **With the Public:** | | | | | | |
| Accrued annual leave | $ | 510 | $ | - | $ | 510 |
| Actuarial FECA liability | | - | | 495 | | 495 |
| Accrued payroll and benefits | | 151 | | - | | 151 |
| Accrued expenses | | 246 | | - | | 246 |
| Liability for deposit funds, clearing accounts and custodial liabilities | | 484 | | - | | 484 |
| Accounts payable | | 12 | | - | | 12 |
| **Other liabilities** | **$** | **1,403** | **$** | **495** | **$** | **1,898** |

| (In Millions) | | 2012 | | | | |
|---|---|---|---|---|---|---|
| | | Current | | Non-Current | | Total |
| **Intragovernmental:** | | | | | | |
| Accrued payroll and benefits | $ | 104 | $ | - | $ | 104 |
| Accrued FECA liability | | 44 | | 55 | | 99 |
| Accrued expenses | | 51 | | - | | 51 |
| **Other liabilities** | **$** | **199** | **$** | **55** | **$** | **254** |
| | | | | | | |
| **With the Public:** | | | | | | |
| Accrued annual leave | $ | 529 | $ | - | $ | 529 |
| Actuarial FECA liability | | - | | 462 | | 462 |
| Accrued payroll and benefits | | 395 | | - | | 395 |
| Accrued expenses | | 201 | | - | | 201 |
| Liability for deposit funds, clearing accounts and custodial liabilities | | 497 | | - | | 497 |
| Accounts payable | | 37 | | - | | 37 |
| **Other liabilities** | **$** | **1,659** | **$** | **462** | **$** | **2,121** |

20

# INTERNAL REVENUE SERVICE

Notes to the Financial Statements

For the Years Ended September 30, 2013 and 2012

## Liabilities Not Covered by Budgetary Resources

| (In Millions) | 2013 | | 2012 | |
| --- | --- | --- | --- | --- |
| | Intra-governmental | With the Public | Intra-governmental | With the Public |
| Accrued annual leave | $ - | $ 510 | $ - | $ 529 |
| Actuarial FECA liability | - | 495 | - | 462 |
| Accrued FECA liability | 99 | - | 99 | - |
| Liabilities not covered by budgetary resources | $ 99 | $ 1,005 | $ 99 | $ 991 |

Liabilities not covered by budgetary resources include liabilities requiring congressional action before budgetary resources can be provided. Although future appropriations to fund these liabilities are likely, it is not certain appropriations will be enacted to fund these liabilities.

**Note 9.** **Leases**

### Capital Leases

The IRS leases ADP telecommunications equipment for toll free call centers, and currently has a two-year lease and two seven-year leases.

The remaining liability on the two-year lease was paid in FY12, and title for the equipment remains with the vendor. The payments for the leased equipment under the seven-year leases were made at the beginning of the leases. There are no future payments due for the equipment under the seven-year leases.

### Operating Leases

| (In Millions) Fiscal Year | Lease Payment |
| --- | --- |
| 2014 | $ 13 |
| 2015 | 12 |
| 2016 | 12 |
| 2017 | 10 |
| 2018 | 6 |
| After 2018 | 1 |
| Total future lease payments | $ 54 |

The IRS leases office space from commercial entities under five-year non-cancelable operating leases. Future lease payments under non-cancelable leases of office spaces are presented above.

Additionally, the IRS has annual operating leases with the General Services Administration for office space and vehicles, and with commercial entities for equipment and software licenses. These leases may be canceled or renewed on an annual basis at the option of the IRS. They do not impose binding commitments on the IRS for future rental payments on leases with terms longer than one year.

21

**INTERNAL REVENUE SERVICE**

Notes to the Financial Statements

For the Years Ended September 30, 2013 and 2012

**Note 10.  Commitments and Contingencies**

The IRS is a party to legal actions whose outcome, if unfavorable, could materially affect the financial statements. Management has determined it is probable one of these proceedings will result in a loss. As of September 30, 2013, the potential damages for this case could be up to $10 million.

For some of the legal actions to which the IRS is a party, management and legal counsel cannot determine the likelihood of an unfavorable outcome nor can any related loss be reasonably estimated. The IRS does not accrue for possible losses related to cases where the potential loss cannot be estimated or the likelihood of an unfavorable outcome is less than probable. As of September 30, 2013 and 2012, there were ten cases and three cases, respectively, for which management and legal counsel are unable to determine the likelihood of an unfavorable outcome or establish a range of potential losses. Two of these cases were filed in the U.S. District Court in which the plaintiffs seek actual and punitive damages in connection with the IRS' alleged unlawful requests for information and unreasonable delays in processing the plaintiffs' applications for tax exempt status. The IRS is also involved in employment related legal actions (e.g., matters alleging discrimination and other claims before federal courts, the Equal Employment Opportunity Commission, the Merit Systems Protection Board, arbitrators, etc.).

For some of these actions, management and legal counsel have determined the likelihood of an unfavorable outcome is remote. As of September 30, 2013 and 2012, there were no estimated contingent liabilities arising from these actions.

As of September 30, 2013 and 2012, the IRS does not have contractual commitments for payments on obligations related to canceled appropriations or contractual arrangements for which the IRS has not recognized liabilities for goods and services provided.

22

# INTERNAL REVENUE SERVICE

Notes to the Financial Statements

For the Years Ended September 30, 2013 and 2012

## Note 11. Cost and Earned Revenue by Programs

| (In Millions) | Taxpayer Assistance and Education | Filing and Account Services | Compliance | Administration of Tax Credit Programs | Total |
|---|---|---|---|---|---|
| | | | **2013** | | |
| Intragovernmental gross cost | $ 150 | $ 1,699 | $ 2,516 | $ 43 | $ 4,408 |
| Gross costs with the public | 457 | 2,130 | 5,680 | 126 | 8,393 |
| Program costs | 607 | 3,829 | 8,196 | 169 | 12,801 |
| Intragovernmental earned revenue | (1) | (50) | (44) | - | (95) |
| Earned revenue from the public | - | (63) | (340) | - | (403) |
| Program revenues | (1) | (113) | (384) | - | (498) |
| Net cost of operations | $ 606 | $ 3,716 | $ 7,812 | $ 169 | $ 12,303 |

| (In Millions) | Taxpayer Assistance and Education | Filing and Account Services | Compliance | Administration of Tax Credit Programs | Total |
|---|---|---|---|---|---|
| | | | **2012** | | |
| Intragovernmental gross cost | $ 278 | $ 1,503 | $ 2,567 | $ 47 | $ 4,395 |
| Gross costs with the public | 647 | 2,068 | 6,005 | 133 | 8,853 |
| Program costs | 925 | 3,571 | 8,572 | 180 | 13,248 |
| Intragovernmental earned revenue | (9) | (28) | (39) | - | (76) |
| Earned revenue from the public | - | (56) | (351) | - | (407) |
| Program revenues | (9) | (84) | (390) | - | (483) |
| Net cost of operations | $ 916 | $ 3,487 | $ 8,182 | $ 180 | $ 12,765 |

23

**INTERNAL REVENUE SERVICE**

Notes to the Financial Statements

For the Years Ended September 30, 2013 and 2012

### Note 12. Statement of Budgetary Resources

**Obligations Incurred**

| (In Millions) | 2013 | 2012 |
|---|---|---|
| **Direct** | | |
| Category B | $ 11,634 | $ 12,105 |
| Exempt from apportionment | 1 | - |
| Total | 11,635 | 12,105 |
| **Reimbursable** | | |
| Category B | 95 | 123 |
| **Obligations Incurred** | $ 11,730 | $ 12,228 |

Category B apportionments distribute budgetary resources by activities or programs and are restricted by purpose for which obligations can be incurred.

**Explanation of Differences Between the FY 2012 Statement of Budgetary Resources and the FY 2014 President's Budget**

| (In Millions) | Budgetary Resources | Obligations Incurred | Distributed Offsetting Receipts | Net Outlays |
|---|---|---|---|---|
| **Statement of Budgetary Resources (SBR)** | $ 13,211 | $ 12,228 | $ 297 | $ 11,775 |
| **Included on SBR, not in President's Budget** | | | | |
| Expired funds | (325) | - | - | - |
| Distributed offsetting receipts | - | - | (297) | 297 |
| Allocation transfer from Treasury | (2) | (1) | - | - |
| Other | (1) | (5) | - | (1) |
| **Included in President's Budget, not on SBR** | | | | |
| Tax credits and interest refunds to taxpayers | 91,475 | 91,475 | - | 91,474 |
| Payments to informants | 94 | 93 | - | 93 |
| **Budget of the United States Government** | $ 104,452 | $ 103,790 | $ - | $ 103,638 |

The *FY 2015 Budget of the United States Government* (President's Budget) presenting the actual amounts for the year ended September 30, 2013 has not been published as of the issue date of these financial statements. The FY 2015 President's Budget is scheduled for publication in February 2014. A reconciliation of the FY 2012 column on the Statement of Budgetary Resources (SBR) to the actual amounts for FY 2012 in the FY 2014 President's Budget for budgetary resources, obligations incurred, distributed offsetting receipts, and net outlays is presented above.

The President's Budget includes $91.6 billion in appropriations for tax credits and interest refunds, and payments to informants. The majority of the appropriations represent budgetary resources and outlays of payments to taxpayers for credits exceeding the taxpayer's income tax liability, including EITC, Child Tax Credit, and Making Work Pay Credit.

24

# INTERNAL REVENUE SERVICE

Notes to the Financial Statements

For the Years Ended September 30, 2013 and 2012

### Undelivered Orders at the End of Period

Undelivered orders are the value of goods and services ordered and obligated, but not yet received. This amount includes any prepaid or advanced orders for which delivery or performance has not yet occurred. Undelivered orders were $847 million and $958 million for the periods ended September 30, 2013 and 2012, respectively.

### Note 13. Collections of Federal Tax Revenue

| (In Billions) | Tax Year 2013 | | Tax Year 2012 | Tax Year 2011 | Prior Years | Collections Received FY 2013 | Collections Received FY 2012 |
|---|---|---|---|---|---|---|---|
| Individual income, FICA/SECA, and other | $ 1,581 | * | $ 822 | $ 22 | $ 24 | $ 2,449 | $ 2,160 |
| Corporate income | 218 | ** | 83 | 2 | 9 | 312 | 282 |
| Excise | 44 | | 17 | - | - | 61 | 56 |
| Estate and gift | * | | 10 | 1 | 9 | 20 | 14 |
| Railroad retirement | 4 | | 1 | - | - | 5 | 5 |
| Federal unemployment | 4 | | 4 | - | - | 8 | 7 |
| Collections of federal tax revenue | $ 1,851 | | $ 937 | $ 25 | $ 42 | $ 2,855 | $ 2,524 |

\* Includes other collections of $301 million.
\*\* Includes tax year 2014 corporate income tax receipts of $14 billion.

### Note 14. Federal Tax Refund Activity

| (In Billions) | Tax Year 2013 | Tax Year 2012 | Tax Year 2011 | Prior Years | Refunds Disbursed FY 2013 | Refunds Disbursed FY 2012 |
|---|---|---|---|---|---|---|
| Individual income, FICA/SECA, and other | $ 1 | $ 287 | $ 22 | $ 11 | $ 321 | $ 328 |
| Corporate income | 5 | 13 | 7 | 16 | 41 | 44 |
| Excise | - | 1 | - | - | 1 | 1 |
| Estate and gift | - | - | - | 1 | 1 | - |
| Federal tax refund activity | $ 6 | $ 301 | $ 29 | $ 28 | $ 364 | $ 373 |

Refund disbursements include payments for various refundable credits including EITC, child tax credit, and those enacted under the ARRA.

25

## INTERNAL REVENUE SERVICE

Notes to the Financial Statements

For the Years Ended September 30, 2013 and 2012

### Note 15.  Fiduciary Activities

| (In Millions) | 2013 | | | | |
| --- | --- | --- | --- | --- | --- |
| | 20X6737 | 20X6738 | 20X6740 | 20X6741 | Total |
| Fiduciary net assets, beginning of year | $    - | $    27 | $    - | $    - | $    27 |
| Contributions | 10 | 13 | 18 | 8 | 49 |
| Disbursements to and on behalf of Beneficiaries | (10) | (7) | (18) | (8) | (43) |
| Increase (decrease) in fiduciary net Assets | - | 6 | - | - | 6 |
| Fiduciary net assets, end of year | $    - | $    33 | $    - | $    - | $    33 |

| (In Millions) | 2012 | | | | |
| --- | --- | --- | --- | --- | --- |
| | 20X6737 | 20X6738 | 20X6740 | 20X6741 | Total |
| Fiduciary net assets, beginning of year | $    - | $    38 | $    - | $    - | $    38 |
| Contributions | 8 | 17 | 44 | 7 | 76 |
| Disbursements to and on behalf of Beneficiaries | (8) | (28) | (44) | (7) | (87) |
| Increase (decrease) in fiduciary net Assets | - | (11) | - | - | (11) |
| Fiduciary net assets, end of year | $    - | $    27 | $    - | $    - | $    27 |

In fiduciary fund 20X6738, the fiduciary net assets, end of year balances are pending a tax matter resolution.

In accordance with the Statement of Federal Financial Accounting Standards No. 31, *Accounting for Fiduciary Activities*, fiduciary cash and other assets are not assets of the Federal Government. The IRS has four fiduciary funds not reported on the balance sheet:

- Internal Revenue Collections for Northern Mariana Islands    20X6737
- Coverover Withholdings – U.S. Virgin Islands    20X6738
- Coverover Withholdings – Guam    20X6740
- Coverover Withholdings – American Samoa    20X6741

Internal Revenue Code (26 USC) Section 7654 governs the tax coordination between the governments of the United States and the U.S. territories of the Northern Mariana Islands, the U.S. Virgin Islands, Guam, and American Samoa.

The collections of federal income taxes withheld from U.S. military and federal employees working in these U.S. territories are maintained in fiduciary funds of the IRS. The disbursements of these collections to these U.S. territory governments represent the transfer of the individual tax liability for a taxable year.

26

## INTERNAL REVENUE SERVICE

Notes to the Financial Statements

For the Years Ended September 30, 2013 and 2012

### Note 16. Reconciliation of Net Cost of Operations to Budget

| (In Millions) | 2013 | 2012 |
|---|---|---|
| **Resources used to finance activities:** | | |
| Obligations incurred | $ 11,730 | $ 12,228 |
| Spending authority from offsetting collections and recoveries | (258) | (249) |
| Distributed offsetting receipts | (333) | (297) |
| Transfers to General Fund | (48) | (51) |
| Imputed financing | 1,272 | 1,191 |
| Transfers in/out without reimbursement | - | 30 |
| | 12,363 | 12,852 |
| **Resources that do not fund net cost of operations:** | | |
| Changes in goods, services and benefits ordered but not yet received or provided | 105 | 35 |
| Costs capitalized on the balance sheet | (170) | (221) |
| Budgetary offsetting collections and receipts | 35 | (17) |
| | (30) | (203) |
| **Costs that do not require resources in current period:** | | |
| Depreciation and amortization | 261 | 304 |
| Increase (decrease) in unfunded liabilities | 13 | 8 |
| Revaluation of assets and liabilities | 14 | 27 |
| Other | (318) | (223) |
| | (30) | 116 |
| **Net cost of operations** | $ 12,303 | $ 12,765 |

In accordance with the Statement of Federal Financial Accounting Standards No. 7, *Accounting for Revenue and Other Financing Sources and Concepts for Reconciling Budgetary and Financial Accounting,* the budgetary resources obligated during the period for the programs and operations of the IRS must be reconciled to the net cost of operations. Budgetary accounting reports the obligations and outlays of financial resources to acquire or provide goods and services. The accrual basis of accounting reports the net cost of resources used.

27

# Required Supplementary Information

---

**INTERNAL REVENUE SERVICE**

Required Supplementary Information - Unaudited

For the Years Ended September 30, 2013 and 2012

## Schedule of Budgetary Resources by Major Budget Accounts

| (In Millions) | Taxpayer Services | | Enforcement | | Operations Support | | Other | | Total | |
|---|---|---|---|---|---|---|---|---|---|---|
| **Budgetary resources** | | | | | | | | | | |
| Unobligated balance, brought forward, October 1 | $ | 62 | $ | 85 | $ | 356 | $ | 480 | $ | 983 |
| Recoveries of prior year unpaid obligations | | 19 | | 25 | | 87 | | 6 | | 137 |
| Other changes in unobligated balance | | 178 | | 9 | | 80 | | (339) | | (72) |
| Unobligated balance from prior year budget authority, net | | 259 | | 119 | | 523 | | 147 | | 1,048 |
| Appropriations (disc & mand) | | 2,136 | | 4,949 | | 3,859 | | 611 | | 11,555 |
| Spending authority from offsetting collections (disc & mand) | | 42 | | 50 | | 27 | | 2 | | 121 |
| **Total budgetary resources** | $ | 2,437 | $ | 5,118 | $ | 4,409 | $ | 760 | $ | 12,724 |
| **Status of budgetary resources** | | | | | | | | | | |
| Obligations incurred | $ | 2,372 | $ | 5,014 | $ | 4,084 | $ | 260 | $ | 11,730 |
| Unobligated balance, end of year: | | | | | | | | | | |
| Apportioned | | 16 | | 30 | | 138 | | 451 | | 635 |
| Exempt from apportionment | | - | | - | | - | | 7 | | 7 |
| Unapportioned | | 49 | | 74 | | 187 | | 42 | | 352 |
| Total unobligated balance, end of year | | 65 | | 104 | | 325 | | 500 | | 994 |
| **Total budgetary resources** | $ | 2,437 | $ | 5,118 | $ | 4,409 | $ | 760 | $ | 12,724 |
| **Change in obligated balance** | | | | | | | | | | |
| Unpaid obligations, brought forward, October 1 (gross) | $ | 204 | $ | 448 | $ | 886 | $ | 135 | $ | 1,673 |
| Obligations incurred | | 2,372 | | 5,014 | | 4,084 | | 260 | | 11,730 |
| Outlays (gross) | | (2,456) | | (5,204) | | (4,021) | | (289) | | (11,970) |
| Recoveries of prior year unpaid obligations | | (19) | | (25) | | (87) | | (6) | | (137) |
| Unpaid obligations, end of year (gross) | | 101 | | 233 | | 862 | | 100 | | 1,296 |
| Uncollected payments, federal sources, brought forward, October 1 | | - | | (34) | | (8) | | - | | (42) |
| Change in uncollected customer payments from federal sources | | - | | 3 | | 8 | | - | | 11 |
| Uncollected payments, federal sources, end of year | | - | | (31) | | - | | - | | (31) |
| Memorandum (non-add) entries: | | | | | | | | | | |
| Obligated balance, start of year (net), as adjusted | | 204 | | 414 | | 878 | | 135 | | 1,631 |
| **Obligated balance, end of year, net** | $ | 101 | $ | 202 | $ | 862 | $ | 100 | $ | 1,265 |
| **Budget authority and outlays, net** | | | | | | | | | | |
| Budget authority, gross (disc & mand) | $ | 2,178 | $ | 4,999 | $ | 3,886 | $ | 613 | $ | 11,676 |
| Actual offsetting collections (disc & mand) | | (42) | | (53) | | (35) | | (2) | | (132) |
| Change in uncollected customer payments from federal sources (disc) | | - | | 3 | | 8 | | - | | 11 |
| **Budget authority, net (disc & mand)** | $ | 2,136 | $ | 4,949 | $ | 3,859 | $ | 611 | $ | 11,555 |
| Outlays, gross (disc & mand) | $ | 2,456 | $ | 5,204 | $ | 4,021 | $ | 289 | $ | 11,970 |
| Actual offsetting collections (disc & mand) | | (42) | | (53) | | (35) | | (2) | | (132) |
| Outlays, net (disc & mand) | | 2,414 | | 5,151 | | 3,986 | | 287 | | 11,838 |
| Distributed offsetting receipts | | - | | - | | - | | (333) | | (333) |
| **Agency outlays, net (disc & mand)** | $ | 2,414 | $ | 5,151 | $ | 3,986 | $ | (46) | $ | 11,505 |

28

# INTERNAL REVENUE SERVICE

Required Supplementary Information - Unaudited

For the Years Ended September 30, 2013 and 2012

## Schedule of Budgetary Resources by Major Budget Accounts

| (In Millions) | Taxpayer Services | | Enforcement | | Operations Support | | Other | | Total | |
|---|---|---|---|---|---|---|---|---|---|---|
| **Budgetary resources** | | | | | | | | | | |
| Unobligated balance, brought forward, October 1 | $ | 69 | $ | 80 | $ | 272 | $ | 469 | $ | 890 |
| Recoveries of prior year unpaid obligations | | 7 | | 21 | | 73 | | 7 | | 108 |
| Other changes in unobligated balance | | 162 | | (10) | | 26 | | (274) | | (96) |
| Unobligated balance from prior year budget authority, net | | 238 | | 91 | | 371 | | 202 | | 902 |
| Appropriations (disc & mand) | | 2,240 | | 5,302 | | 3,997 | | 629 | | 12,168 |
| Spending authority from offsetting collections (disc & mand) | | 28 | | 69 | | 41 | | 3 | | 141 |
| **Total budgetary resources** | $ | 2,506 | $ | 5,452 | $ | 4,409 | $ | 834 | $ | 13,211 |
| **Status of budgetary resources** | | | | | | | | | | |
| Obligations incurred | $ | 2,444 | $ | 5,377 | $ | 4,053 | $ | 354 | $ | 12,228 |
| Unobligated balance, end of year: | | | | | | | | | | |
| Apportioned | | 17 | | 29 | | 186 | | 366 | | 598 |
| Exempt from apportionment | | - | | - | | - | | 7 | | 7 |
| Unapportioned | | 45 | | 56 | | 170 | | 107 | | 378 |
| Total unobligated balance, end of year | | 62 | | 85 | | 356 | | 480 | | 983 |
| **Total budgetary resources** | $ | 2,506 | $ | 5,452 | $ | 4,409 | $ | 834 | $ | 13,211 |
| **Change in obligated balance** | | | | | | | | | | |
| Unpaid obligations, brought forward, October 1 (gross) | $ | 191 | $ | 482 | $ | 949 | $ | 155 | $ | 1,777 |
| Obligations incurred | | 2,444 | | 5,377 | | 4,053 | | 354 | | 12,228 |
| Outlays (gross) | | (2,424) | | (5,390) | | (4,043) | | (367) | | (12,224) |
| Recoveries of prior year unpaid obligations | | (7) | | (21) | | (73) | | (7) | | (108) |
| Unpaid obligations, end of year (gross) | | 204 | | 448 | | 886 | | 135 | | 1,673 |
| Uncollected payments, federal sources, brought forward, October 1 | | - | | (44) | | (9) | | - | | (53) |
| Change in uncollected customer payments from federal sources | | - | | 10 | | 1 | | - | | 11 |
| Uncollected payments, federal sources, end of year | | - | | (34) | | (8) | | - | | (42) |
| Memorandum (non-add) entries | | | | | | | | | | |
| Obligated balance, start of year (net), as adjusted | | 191 | | 438 | | 940 | | 155 | | 1,724 |
| **Obligated balance, end of year, net** | $ | 204 | $ | 414 | $ | 878 | $ | 135 | $ | 1,631 |
| **Budget authority and outlays, net** | | | | | | | | | | |
| Budget authority, gross (disc & mand) | $ | 2,268 | $ | 5,371 | $ | 4,038 | $ | 632 | $ | 12,309 |
| Actual offsetting collections (disc & mand) | | (28) | | (79) | | (42) | | (3) | | (152) |
| Change in uncollected customer payments from federal sources (disc) | | - | | 10 | | 1 | | - | | 11 |
| **Budget authority, net (disc & mand)** | $ | 2,240 | $ | 5,302 | $ | 3,997 | $ | 629 | $ | 12,168 |
| Outlays, gross (disc & mand) | $ | 2,424 | $ | 5,390 | $ | 4,043 | $ | 367 | $ | 12,224 |
| Actual offsetting collections (disc & mand) | | (28) | | (79) | | (42) | | (3) | | (152) |
| Outlays, net (disc & mand) | | 2,396 | | 5,311 | | 4,001 | | 364 | | 12,072 |
| Distributed offsetting receipts | | - | | - | | - | | (297) | | (297) |
| **Agency outlays, net (disc & mand)** | $ | 2,396 | $ | 5,311 | $ | 4,001 | $ | 67 | $ | 11,775 |

29

**INTERNAL REVENUE SERVICE**

Required Supplementary Information - Unaudited

For the Years Ended September 30, 2013 and 2012

## Other Claims for Refunds

Management has estimated amounts that may be paid out as other claims for tax refunds. This estimate represents an amount (principal and interest), which may be paid for claims pending judicial review by the federal courts or, internally, by Appeals. In FY 2013, the total estimated payout (including principal and interest) for claims pending judicial review by the federal courts is $0.8 billion and by Appeals is $3.5 billion. In FY 2012, the total estimated payout (including principal and interest) for claims pending judicial review by the federal courts was $6.1 billion and by Appeals was $5.3 billion. To the extent judgments against the government in these cases prompt other similarly situated taxpayers to file similar refund claims, these amounts could become significantly greater.

The Treasury Department made an administrative determination to accept the position that certain medical residents who received stipends be exempted from Federal Insurance Contributions Act taxes for periods before April 1, 2005. As of September 30, 2013 and 2012, the IRS has estimated unpaid refund claims of approximately $0.1 billion and $2.4 billion, respectively.

In accordance with federal accounting standards, these claims have not been recorded in the financial statements because certain administrative processes had not yet been completed by the end of FY 2013.

## Federal Taxes Receivable, Net

In accordance with the Statement of Federal Financial Accounting Standards No. 7, *Accounting for Revenue and Other Financing Sources and Concepts for Reconciling Budgetary and Financial Accounting*, some unpaid assessments do not meet the criteria for financial statement recognition as discussed in Note 1.F., Federal Taxes Receivable, Net and Due to Treasury. Although compliance assessments and write-offs are not considered receivables under federal accounting standards, they represent legally enforceable claims of the IRS acting on behalf of the Federal Government. There is, however, a significant difference in the collection potential of these categories.

The components of the total unpaid assessments and derivation of net federal taxes receivable were as follows:

| (In Billions) | 2013 | | 2012 | |
|---|---|---|---|---|
| Total unpaid assessments | $ | 374 | $ | 364 |
| Compliance assessments | | (85) | | (87) |
| Write-offs | | (130) | | (125) |
| **Gross federal taxes receivables** | | 159 | | 152 |
| Allowance for uncollectible taxes receivable | | (124) | | (113) |
| **Federal taxes receivable, net** | **$** | **35** | **$** | **39** |

Total unpaid assessments in FY 2012 included $2 billion of Branded Prescription Drug fees, which were collected in FY 2013.

30

**INTERNAL REVENUE SERVICE**

Required Supplementary Information - Unaudited

For the Years Ended September 30, 2013 and 2012

To eliminate double-counting, the compliance assessments reported above exclude trust fund recovery penalties assessed against officers and directors of businesses involved in the non-remittance of federal taxes withheld from their employees. These penalties totaled $2 billion as of September 30, 2013 and September 30, 2012. The related unpaid assessments of those businesses are reported as taxes receivable or write-offs, but the IRS may also recover portions of those businesses' unpaid assessments from any and all individual officers and directors against whom a trust fund recovery penalty is assessed.

The IRS cannot reasonably estimate the allowance for uncollectible amounts pertaining to its compliance assessments, and thus cannot determine their net realizable value or the value of the pre-assessment work-in-process.

31

# Other Information

**INTERNAL REVENUE SERVICE**

Other Information - Unaudited

For the Years Ended September 30, 2013 and 2012

## Schedule of Spending

The Schedule of Spending (SOS) presented below is an overview of the fiscal year (FY) 2013 resources of the Internal Revenue Service (IRS) and how they were used. The schedule is presented to help the public better understand what money was provided to the IRS, how the IRS spent the money, and to whom the money was paid.

The data used to populate this schedule is the same underlying data used to populate the Statement of Budgetary Resources (SBR). The amounts shown below as "Total amounts agreed to be spent" agree with amounts shown as "Obligations, incurred" on the SBR.

The underlying data for this schedule also populates the information on USASPENDING.GOV, which was established to provide a single searchable website accessible to the public at no cost. USASPENDING.GOV receives and displays data pertaining to obligations incurred by the Agency, but there are known differences between the website and the SBR. Most notably, the website does not contain obligations incurred for individuals (e.g., payroll expenses) or for transactions less than $25,000.

| (In Millions) | | 2013 |
|---|---|---|
| **What money is available to spend?** | | |
| Total resources | $ | 12,724 |
| Less amount available but not agreed to be spent | | (642) |
| Less amount not available to be spent | | (352) |
| **Total amounts agreed to be spent** | $ | 11,730 |
| **How was the money spent/issued?** | | |
| Tax administration | | |
| Personnel compensation | $ | 6,482 |
| Personnel benefits | | 2,092 |
| Rent, communications and utilities | | 1,021 |
| Contracts | | 1,529 |
| Other | | 606 |
| **Total amounts agreed to be spent** | $ | 11,730 |
| **Who did the money go to?** | | |
| Federal | $ | 3,104 |
| Non Federal | | 8,626 |
| **Total amounts agreed to be spent** | $ | 11,730 |

32

# INTERNAL REVENUE SERVICE

Other Information - Unaudited

For the Years Ended September 30, 2013 and 2012

## Refundable Tax Credits and Other Outlays

To offer tax relief to targeted individuals and businesses, Congress has provided assistance in the form of tax credits. For the majority of tax credits, the economic benefit is limited to the taxpayer's tax liability. Credits limited in this manner are termed nonrefundable credits. Refundable credits, in contrast, are fully payable to the taxpayer, even if the credit exceeds the tax liability. These types of credits provide greater economic benefits because the taxpayer realizes the full benefit of the credit, regardless of the underlying tax liability.

The following overview summarizes the refundable credits the IRS administers and pays. The overview describes refundable credits in existence for many years, as well as those enacted as part of the *American Recovery and Reinvestment Act of 2009* (ARRA) and the *Patient Protection and Affordable Care Act of 2010* (PPACA).

### Earned Income Tax Credit

The Earned Income Tax Credit (EITC) is a refundable tax credit for low to moderate income working individuals and families. Congress originally approved the tax credit legislation in 1975, in part, to offset the burden of social security taxes and to provide an incentive to work. To qualify, taxpayers must meet certain requirements and file a tax return, even if they did not have sufficient income to meet regular tax return filing requirements.

### Additional Child Tax Credit

The Additional Child Tax Credit is a special credit for taxpayers who work, have earnings below an established ceiling, and have a qualifying child. The Child Tax Credit is limited to the taxpayer's tax liability and is a nonrefundable tax credit. However, certain individuals who receive less than the full amount of the Child Tax Credit may qualify for the "Additional" Child Tax Credit. Under this credit, subject to additional criteria, the taxpayer may receive the full credit amount even if such amount exceeds the taxpayer's tax liability. Consequently, the Additional Child Tax Credit is categorized as a refundable tax credit.

### Health Care Tax Credit

The Health Care Tax Credit was established in 2002 to assist economically dislocated workers in acquiring or continuing critical health care coverage during periods of economic distress. Under this credit, participants can elect to take a portion of their premium as a credit on their tax return.

Alternatively, participants can elect to receive direct reimbursements should they have insufficient tax liability against which to apply the credit.

### Individual Alternative Minimum Tax (AMT) Credit

In 2007, the Individual Alternative Minimum Tax (AMT) Credit was established. This refundable credit is calculated by referencing specific timing items that produced an AMT liability in earlier years. Timing items involve certain transactions, such as incentive stock options and adjustments for accelerated depreciation. Non timing events, such as having a large number of exemptions or a large itemized deduction for state and local taxes, will not qualify for the credit.

33

## INTERNAL REVENUE SERVICE

Other Information - Unaudited

For the Years Ended September 30, 2013 and 2012

### First-Time Home Buyer Credit

In 2008, Congress provided taxpayers with a refundable tax credit equivalent to an interest-free loan equal to ten percent of the purchase price of a home (up to $7,500) by a first-time home buyer. The provision applied to homes purchased on or after April 9, 2008, and before July 1, 2009. Taxpayers receiving this tax credit are required to repay any amount received under this provision back to the government over 15 years in equal installments, or earlier if the home is sold. The credit phases out for taxpayers with adjusted gross income in excess of $75,000 ($150,000 in the case of a joint return).

The ARRA bill eliminated the repayment obligation for taxpayers who purchase homes after January 1, 2009, increased the maximum value of the credit to $8,000, and removed the prohibition on financing by mortgage revenue bonds. Additionally, ARRA extended the availability of the credit for homes purchased before December 1, 2009. The ARRA provision retains the credit recapture if the house is sold within three years of purchase.

### Corporate Alternative Minimum Tax (AMT) Credit

Section 168(k)(4) allows a taxpayer to elect to claim a refundable credit for certain unused research credits in lieu of the special depreciation allowance for eligible property.

### American Opportunity Tax Credit

The American Opportunity Tax Credit modifies the existing Hope Credit. The credit was extended to apply for tax years through 2017 by the *American Taxpayer Relief Act of 2012*. This tax credit makes the Hope Credit available to a broader range of taxpayers including many with higher incomes and those who owe no tax. Additionally, it adds required course materials to the list of qualifying expenses and allows the credit to be claimed for four post-secondary education years instead of two. Many of those eligible will qualify for the maximum annual credit of $2,500 per student.

### Making Work Pay Credit

The Making Work Pay Credit was established in 2009. This is a refundable tax credit calculated at a rate of 6.2 percent of earned income, phasing out for taxpayers with adjusted gross income in excess of $75,000 ($150,000 for married couples filing jointly). Taxpayers receive this benefit through a reduction in the amount of income tax withheld from their paychecks or through claiming the credit on their tax returns.

### Build America and Recovery Zone Bonds (BAB)

BABs are a financing tool for state and local governments. The bonds, which allow a new direct federal payment subsidy, are taxable bonds issued by state and local governments to give them access to the conventional corporate debt markets. At the election of the state and local governments, the U.S. Department of Treasury (Treasury) will make a direct payment to the state or local governmental issuer in an amount equal to 35 percent of the interest payment on the Build America Bonds. This federal subsidy payment provides state and local governments lower net borrowing costs and allows them to reach more sources of borrowing than they can with more traditional tax-exempt or tax credit bonds.

34

## INTERNAL REVENUE SERVICE

Other Information - Unaudited

For the Years Ended September 30, 2013 and 2012

Created by the ARRA, Recovery Zone Bonds are targeted to areas particularly affected by job losses and help local governments obtain financing for much needed economic development projects, such as public infrastructure development.

### Qualified Zone Academy Bonds (QZAB) and Qualified School Construction Bonds (QSCB)

Congress created QZABs and QSCBs to help schools raise funds to renovate and repair buildings, invest in equipment and current technology, develop more challenging curricula, and train teachers. The tax credit portion of these bonds depends on the issuance date of the bonds, the number of bonds outstanding, and their redemption.

### Qualified Energy Conservation and New Clean Renewable Energy Bonds

Qualified Energy Conservation Bonds (QECB) may be issued by state, local, and tribal governments to finance qualified energy conservation projects. A minimum of 70 percent of a state's allocation must be used for governmental purposes, and the remainder may be used to finance private activity projects. QECBs were originally structured as tax credit bonds. However, the March 2010 *Hiring Incentives to Restore Employment* (HIRE) *Act* (H.R. 2847 (Sec. 301)) changed QECB from tax credit bonds to direct subsidy bonds similar to BABs. The QECB issuer pays the investor a taxable coupon and receives a rebate from Treasury.

New Clean Renewable Energy Bonds (CREBs) may be issued by public power utilities, electric cooperatives, government entities (states, cities, counties, territories, Indian tribal governments), and certain lenders to finance renewable energy projects. CREBs were originally structured as tax credit bonds. However, the March 2010 HIRE Act (H.R. 2847 (Sec. 301)) changed CREBs from tax credit bonds to direct subsidy bonds similar to BABs. The issuer pays the investor a taxable coupon and receives a rebate from Treasury.

### COBRA Continuation Coverage for Unemployed Workers

To assist persons in maintaining health coverage for themselves and their families, ARRA provides a 65 percent subsidy for COBRA continuation premiums for up to nine months for workers who have been involuntarily terminated. Additionally, this subsidy applies to health care continuation coverage if required by states for small employers.

To qualify for premium assistance, a worker must have been involuntarily terminated between September 1, 2008 and December 31, 2009. The subsidy terminates upon an offer of any new employer-sponsored health care coverage or Medicare eligibility. Workers who were involuntarily terminated between September 1, 2008 and enactment, but failed to initially elect COBRA because it was unaffordable, were given an additional 60 days to elect COBRA and receive the subsidy. To ensure this assistance is targeted at workers who are most in need, participants must attest their same year income will not exceed $125,000 for individuals and $250,000 for families.

COBRA continuation coverage payments to workers are initially paid by the employer. The employer receives reimbursement either as a direct refund or through their payroll tax return where payments are taken as a credit against existing withholdings and payroll taxes.

35

## INTERNAL REVENUE SERVICE

Other Information - Unaudited

For the Years Ended September 30, 2013 and 2012

### Adoption Tax Credit

Individuals qualify for the adoption tax credit if they have adopted a child and paid out-of-pocket expenses relating to the adoption. They may claim an adoption credit of up to $13,360 (for tax year 2011) per eligible child. In tax year 2012, the credit changed from a refundable to a non-refundable credit. The credit is phased out based on the individual's modified adjusted gross income.

### Small Business Insurance Tax Credit

Certain small employers will be eligible for a tax credit, provided they contribute a uniform percentage of at least 50 percent toward their employees' health insurance. For nonprofit (tax-exempt) organizations, the credit will be in the form of a reduction in income and Medicare tax the employer is required to withhold from employees' wages and the employer share of Medicare tax on employees' wages.

### Therapeutic Discovery Grants

The Qualifying Therapeutic Discovery Project tax credit is provided under new Section 48D of the Internal Revenue Code (26 USC), enacted as part of the PPACA. The credit is a tax benefit targeted to certain therapeutic discovery projects. Such projects must show a reasonable potential to (1) achieve new therapies to treat unmet medical needs, (2) detect or treat chronic or acute diseases and conditions, (3) reduce the long-term growth of health care costs, or (4) significantly advance the goal of curing cancer.

36

## INTERNAL REVENUE SERVICE

Other Information - Unaudited

For the Years Ended September 30, 2013 and 2012

The following table summarizes refundable tax credits in excess of tax liabilities and outlays paid in FY 2013 and FY 2012.

| (In Millions) | 2013 | 2012 |
|---|---|---|
| Earned Income Tax Credit | $ 57,513 | $ 54,890 |
| Additional Child Tax Credit | 21,608 | 22,106 |
| Health Care Tax Credit | 121 | 131 |
| Individual Alternative Minimum Tax (AMT) Credit | 169 | 205 |
| First-Time Homebuyer Credit | 17 | 52 |
| Corporate Alternative Minimum Tax (AMT) Credit | 190 | 101 |
| American Opportunity Tax Credit | 4,041 | 5,549 |
| Making Work Pay Credit * | (11) | 253 |
| Build America and Recovery Zone Bonds | 3,899 | 3,749 |
| Qualified Zone Academy Bonds | 51 | 40 |
| Qualified School Construction Bonds | 699 | 634 |
| Clean Renewable Energy Bonds | 29 | 20 |
| Energy Conservation Bonds | 29 | 23 |
| COBRA Credit | 30 | 192 |
| Adoption Credit | 143 | 777 |
| Small Business Health Insurance Tax Credit | 75 | 67 |
| Therapeutic Discovery Grants | - | 7 |
| Credit for Certain Government Retirees * | - | (1) |
| Refundable tax credits | $ 88,603 | $ 88,795 |

* Reflects net return of payments

37

## INTERNAL REVENUE SERVICE

Other Information - Unaudited

For the Years Ended September 30, 2013 and 2012

### Social Security and Medicare Taxes

The Federal Insurance Contributions Act (FICA) provides for a federal system of old-age, survivors, disability, and hospital insurance benefits. Payments to trust funds established for these programs are financed by payroll taxes on employee wages and tips, employers' matching payments, and a tax on self-employment income.

A portion of FICA benefits involves old-age, survivors, and disability payments. These benefits are funded by the social security tax, which is currently 6.2 percent of wages and tips up to $113,700, and an employer matching amount of 6.2 percent, bringing the total rate to 12.4 percent for calendar year 2013. In calendar year 2012, the rate was 4.2 percent of wages and tips up to $110,100 and an employer matching amount of 6.2 percent, bringing the total rate to 10.4 percent. These benefits are also funded by a self-employment tax of 12.4 percent and 10.4 percent on self-employment income up to $113,700, and $110,100 for calendar years 2013 and 2012, respectively. Remaining benefits under FICA pertain to hospital benefits (referred to as "Medicare") and are funded by a separate 1.45 percent tax on all wages and tips (there is no wage limit) and the employer matching contribution of 1.45 percent, bringing the total rate to 2.9 percent. Self-employed individuals pay a Medicare tax of 2.9 percent on all self-employment income. Beginning in 2013, an additional Medicare tax of 0.9 percent was collected on earned individual income of more than $200,000 ($250,000 for married couples filing jointly). Social security taxes collected by the IRS were estimated to be approximately $680 billion and $576 billion in FY 2013 and FY 2012, respectively. Medicare taxes collected by the IRS were estimated to be approximately $211 billion and $203 billion in FY 2013 and FY 2012, respectively. Social security taxes and Medicare taxes are included in the Individual income, FICA/SECA, and other financial statement line on the Statement of Custodial Activity.

### Tax Gap and Tax Burden

#### Tax Gap

The tax gap is the difference between the amount of tax imposed by law and what taxpayers actually pay on time. The tax gap arises from the three types of noncompliance: not filing required tax returns on time or at all (the nonfiling gap), underreporting the correct amount of tax on timely filed returns (the underreporting gap), and not paying on time the full amount reported on timely filed returns (the underpayment gap). Of these three components, only the underpayment gap is observed; the nonfiling gap and the underreporting gap must be estimated. The tax gap, estimated to be about $450 billion for tax year 2006 (the most recent estimate made), represents the net amount of noncompliance with the tax laws. Underreporting of tax liability accounts for 84 percent of the gap, with the remainder divided between nonfiling (6 percent) and underpaying (10 percent). Part of the estimate is based on data from a study of individual returns filed for tax year 2006. It does not include any taxes that should have been paid on income from illegal activities. Each instance of noncompliance by a taxpayer contributes to the tax gap, whether or not the IRS detects it, and whether or not the taxpayer is even aware of the noncompliance. Some of the tax gap arises from intentional (willful) noncompliance, and some of it arises from unintentional mistakes.

The collection gap is the cumulative amount of tax, penalties, and interest assessed over many years, but not paid by a certain point in time, which the IRS expects will remain uncollectible. In essence, it represents the difference between the total balance of unpaid assessments and the net taxes receivable

38

**INTERNAL REVENUE SERVICE**

Other Information - Unaudited

For the Years Ended September 30, 2013 and 2012

reported on the balance sheet of the IRS. The tax gap and the collection gap are related and overlapping concepts, but they have significant differences. The collection gap is a cumulative balance sheet concept for a particular point in time, while the tax gap is like an income statement item for a single year. Moreover, the tax gap estimates include all noncompliance, while the collection gap includes only amounts that have been assessed (a small portion of all noncompliance) and have not yet reached their statutory collection expiration date. Also, the tax gap includes only tax, while the collection gap includes tax, penalties, and interest.

**Tax Burden**

The Internal Revenue Code provides for progressive rates of tax, whereby higher incomes are generally subject to higher rates of tax. The following pages present in both graph and table format various income levels and their associated tax liabilities for individuals and corporations. This information is the most recent available for individuals (tax year 2011) and corporations (tax year 2010). The graphs and charts are representative of more detailed data and analyses available from the IRS Statistics of Income (SOI) office.

For individuals, the information illustrates, in both percentage and dollar terms, the tax burden borne by varying levels of Adjusted Gross Income (AGI). The corporate information illustrates, for varying corporate asset categories, the tax burden borne by these entities as a percentage of taxable income.

**Tax Expenditures**

Total tax expenditures are the foregone federal revenue resulting from deductions and credits provided in the Internal Revenue Code. Since tax expenditures directly affect funds available for government operations, decisions to forego federal revenue are as important as decisions to spend federal revenue.

39

## INTERNAL REVENUE SERVICE

Other Information - Unaudited

For the Years Ended September 30, 2013 and 2012

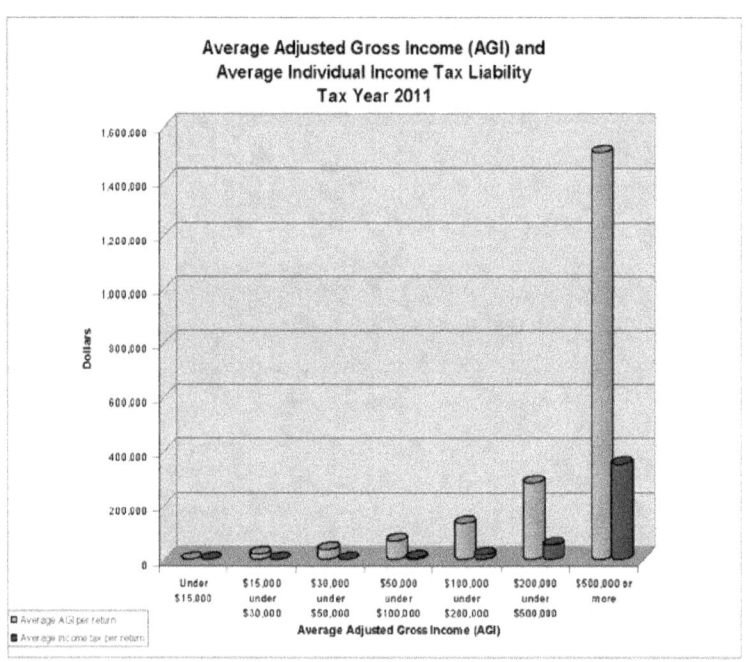

### Average Adjusted Gross Income (AGI) and Average Individual Income Tax Liability Tax Year 2011

| Adjusted gross income (AGI) | Number of taxable returns (in thousands) | AGI (in millions) | Total income tax (in millions) | Average AGI per return (in whole dollars) | Average income tax per return (in whole dollars) | Income tax as a percentage of AGI |
|---|---|---|---|---|---|---|
| Under $15,000 | 38,456 | 87,540 | 2,304 | 2,276 | 60 | 2.6% |
| $15,000 under $30,000 | 31,078 | 682,619 | 19,113 | 21,965 | 615 | 2.8% |
| $30,000 under $50,000 | 25,504 | 996,793 | 55,297 | 39,083 | 2,168 | 5.5% |
| $50,000 under $100,000 | 30,876 | 2,197,423 | 189,342 | 71,169 | 6,132 | 8.6% |
| $100,000 under $200,000 | 14,756 | 1,977,406 | 248,966 | 134,007 | 16,872 | 12.6% |
| $200,000 under $500,000 | 3,802 | 1,080,932 | 212,403 | 284,306 | 55,866 | 19.6% |
| $500,000 or more | 898 | 1,351,440 | 318,094 | 1,504,944 | 354,225 | 23.5% |
| Totals | 145,370 | 8,374,143 | 1,045,511 | - | - | - |

(All figures are estimates and based on samples provided by the Statistics of Income (SOI) Office.)

40

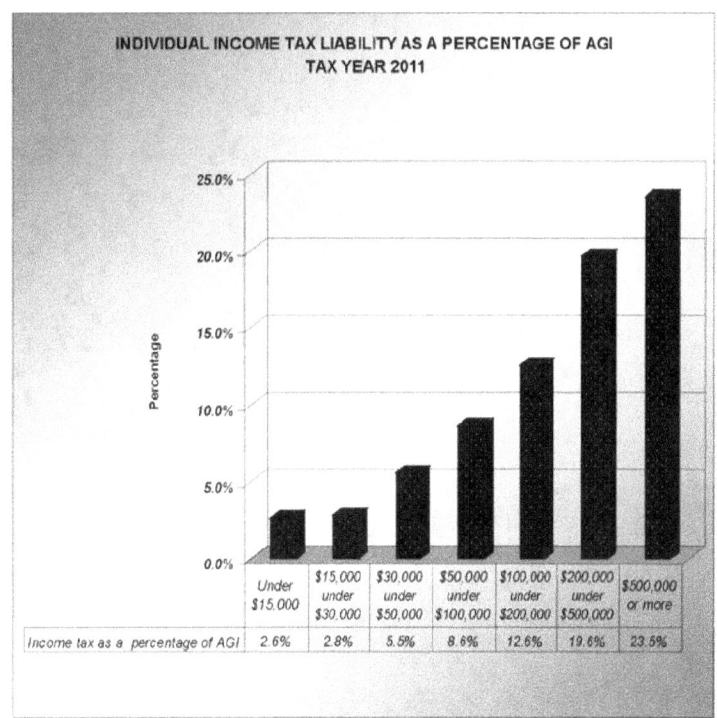

INTERNAL REVENUE SERVICE

Other Information - Unaudited

For the Years Ended September 30, 2013 and 2012

### INDIVIDUAL INCOME TAX LIABILITY AS A PERCENTAGE OF AGI TAX YEAR 2011

| | Under $15,000 | $15,000 under $30,000 | $30,000 under $50,000 | $50,000 under $100,000 | $100,000 under $200,000 | $200,000 under $500,000 | $500,000 or more |
|---|---|---|---|---|---|---|---|
| Income tax as a percentage of AGI | 2.6% | 2.8% | 5.5% | 8.6% | 12.6% | 19.6% | 23.5% |

(All figures are estimates and based on samples provided by the Statistics of Income (SOI) Office.)

41

## INTERNAL REVENUE SERVICE

Other Information - Unaudited

For the Years Ended September 30, 2013 and 2012

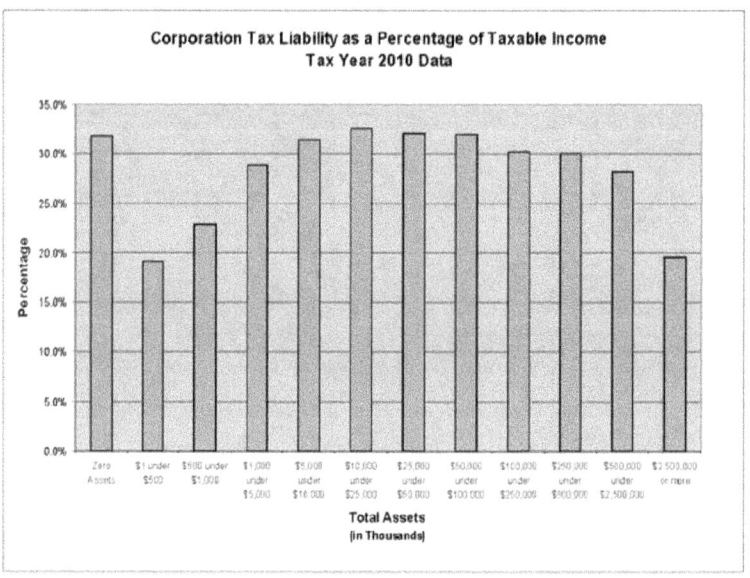

Corporation Tax Liability as a Percentage of Taxable Income
Tax Year 2010 Data

| Total Assets (in thousands) | Income subject to tax (in millions) | Total income tax after credits (in millions) | Percentage of income tax after credits to taxable income |
|---|---|---|---|
| Zero Assets | 15,068 | 4,789 | 31.8% |
| $1 under $500 | 6,167 | 1,178 | 19.1% |
| $500 under $1,000 | 3,231 | 741 | 22.9% |
| $1,000 under $5,000 | 10,274 | 2,970 | 28.9% |
| $5,000 under $10,000 | 6,890 | 2,162 | 31.4% |
| $10,000 under $25,000 | 10,312 | 3,358 | 32.6% |
| $25,000 under $50,000 | 9,900 | 3,175 | 32.1% |
| $50,000 under $100,000 | 12,955 | 4,150 | 32.0% |
| $100,000 under $250,000 | 23,640 | 7,143 | 30.2% |
| $250,000 under $500,000 | 29,057 | 8,732 | 30.1% |
| $500,000 under $2,500,000 | 109,072 | 30,770 | 28.2% |
| $2,500,000 or more | 785,609 | 153,801 | 19.6% |
| **Total** | **1,022,175** | **222,969** | |

(All figures are estimates and based on samples provided by the Statistics of Income (SOI) Office.)

42

# Appendix I: Management's Report on Internal Control over Financial Reporting

**DEPARTMENT OF THE TREASURY**
INTERNAL REVENUE SERVICE
WASHINGTON, D.C. 20224

COMMISSIONER

December 11, 2013

Ms. Cheryl E. Clark
Director, Financial Management and Assurance
U.S. Government Accountability Office
441 G Street, NW, Room 5474
Washington, DC 20548

Dear Ms. Clark:

The Internal Revenue Service's (IRS) internal control over financial reporting is a process effected by those charged with governance, management, and other personnel, the objectives of which are to provide reasonable assurance that: (1) transactions are properly recorded, processed and summarized to permit the preparation of financial statements in accordance with U.S. generally accepted accounting principles, and assets are safeguarded against loss from unauthorized acquisition, use, or disposition; and (2) transactions are executed in accordance with laws governing the use of budget authority and with other applicable laws, regulations, and contracts that could have a direct and material effect on the financial statements.

IRS management is responsible for maintaining effective internal control over financial reporting, including the design, implementation, and maintenance of internal control relevant to the preparation and fair presentation of financial statements that are free from material misstatement, whether due to fraud or error. IRS management evaluated the effectiveness of the IRS's internal control over financial reporting as of September 30, 2013, based on the criteria established under 31 U.S.C. 3512(c), (d) (commonly known as the Federal Managers' Financial Integrity Act).

Based on our evaluation, the IRS has one material weakness in its internal control over financial reporting, specifically unpaid tax assessments. The IRS's financial management systems do not substantially comply with the requirements of the Federal Financial Management Improvement Act. On this basis, management provides qualified assurance that as of September 30, 2013, the IRS's internal control over financial reporting was effective.

Daniel I. Werfel
Acting Commissioner

December 11, 2013
Date

Robin L. Canady
Chief Financial Officer

December 11, 2013
Date

# Appendix II: Comments from the Internal Revenue Service

DEPARTMENT OF THE TREASURY
INTERNAL REVENUE SERVICE
WASHINGTON, D.C. 20224

COMMISSIONER

December 5, 2013

Ms. Cheryl E. Clark
Director
Financial Management and Assurance
U.S. Government Accountability Office
441 G Street, NW, Room 5474
Washington, DC 20548

Dear Ms. Clark:

Thank you for the opportunity to comment on the draft report titled, *Financial Audit: IRS's Fiscal Years 2013 and 2012 Financial Statements*. We are pleased that the Internal Revenue Service (IRS) received an unqualified opinion on the combined financial statements for the 14th consecutive year. The unqualified opinion demonstrates that the IRS accurately accounts for approximately $2.9 trillion in tax revenue receipts, $364 billion in tax refunds, and $11 billion in IRS appropriated funds.

We are pleased the Government Accountability Office (GAO) recognized our progress in addressing a large number of previously reported system control deficiencies and successfully implementing both a new procurement system and an upgrade to our administrative accounting system software as important steps towards improving the overall effectiveness of information system controls. The IRS is dedicated to continuing to improve its financial management, internal controls, and information technology security posture.

I want to recognize the GAO's support throughout the audit. While challenges remain, the IRS has established its ability to consistently produce accurate and reliable financial statements. We have a solid management team dedicated to promoting the highest standard of financial management, and we continue to increase our focus on information security and internal controls. We look forward to working with the GAO in our efforts to continue to improve controls over financial reporting.

Sincerely,

Daniel I. Werfel
Acting Commissioner